THE ESSENTIAL AQUARIUM

THE ESSENTIAL

AQUARIUM

A GUIDE TO KEEPING 100 EXCITING FRESHWATER SPECIES

EDWARD BAUMAN

PHOTOGRAPHS BY AARON NORMAN

J. B. FAIRFAX
LONDON

A FRIEDMAN GROUP BOOK

Published 1991 by J B Fairfax Limited
Ferry House, 51/57 Lacy Road
Putney, London, SW15 1PR

By arrangement with Michael Friedman Publishing Group, Inc.

ISBN 1 85391 296 4

A catalogue record for this book is available from the British Library.

THE ESSENTIAL AQUARIUM
A Guide to Keeping 100 Exciting Freshwater Species
was prepared and produced by
Michael Friedman Publishing Group, Inc.
15 West 26th Street
New York, New York 10010

Editor: Elizabeth Viscott Sullivan
Art Director: Jeff Batzli
Designer: Kingsley Parker
Photography Editor: Christopher C. Bain

Typeset by The Interface Group, Inc.
Colour separation by Excel Graphic Art Co.
Printed and bound in Hong Kong by Leefung-Asco Printers Ltd.

To my wife, Shari, whose interest and
support made this book possible.

CONTENTS

INTRODUCTION

Aquariums are fascinating. Put an aquarium stocked with fish in a living room, the lobby of an office, or the entrance to a restaurant, and people will be drawn to it. It's more than just the interesting colors, shapes, and sizes of aquarium fish that attract so much attention. There is something delightful about the way fish appear to be suspended in their aquatic world, moving easily and gracefully in any direction they choose.

Studies have demonstrated that watching fish in an aquarium is a very relaxing experience. Heart and pulse rates are lowered, and stress seeps away. It's nice to know that aquariums are not only fun but also good for us.

Around the world tens of millions of people keep aquariums. Fortunately, fishkeeping is one of those hobbies that can be enjoyed at many levels of participation. Some hobbyists are quite satisfied to have one 10-gallon (38-l) aquarium stocked with a few plants and small, colorful fish. Then there are other hobbyists who build special rooms that can house dozens or even hundreds of tanks. Sometimes the goal is to specialize in a certain family of fish, other times to breed fish for new colors and patterns or special finnage.

The educational value of fishkeeping is also important. Observing fish in an aquarium offers wonderful opportunities to learn how fish live their lives. The physical traits, behavior, and interactions of fish are revealed to us in ways that are often impossible to discover in their natural environments. At the same time, fishkeeping leads to a greater appreciation of the importance of preserving the natural habitats of fish, which are endangered in many parts of the world, particularly in South America.

Keeping an aquarium or two does not have to be expensive or time consuming, nor does it require a lot of space. When properly set up, an aquarium can be maintained with relatively little effort. The tanks and equipment available today are more reliable than ever, and research into fish nutrition has resulted in a wide variety of high-quality commercial foods.

To be honest, not everyone succeeds in the aquarium hobby. In fact, more than one-half of the people who set up an aquarium for the first time leave the hobby within a year. Although fishkeeping is not particularly difficult, we are not born knowing how to go about it. It does, at first glance, seem relatively simple. Problems with diseased and dying fish, however, eventually force novice fishkeepers to either learn more about the subject or give up their aquariums.

This book is an introduction to aquariums, fish, and fishkeeping. Although biology and chemistry are very much a part of these topics, we will deal with science only as it relates to the purpose of the book, which is to help you successfully set up an aquarium, and avoid the common problems that many new hobbyists encounter. Once you understand how to choose an aquarium and other equipment, how to set up the tank, how to select fish, and how to maintain the aquarium, you will be able to become as involved in the hobby as you wish to.

The first half of this book is devoted to a variety of topics ranging from the aquarium as a closed aquatic environment to step-by-step instructions on how to set the tank up. You will get more from this book if you read it from beginning to end. The discussion of each topic builds on previous topics.

The remainder of the book is given over to photographs and descriptions of the most popular aquarium fish. Although there are hundreds of species of fish available that are suitable for aquariums, many have highly specialized requirements, making them poor choices for new aquarists. The species covered in this book were chosen for their availability and hardiness. All are likely to do well in a community tank as long as the combination of fish chosen is given some thought before purchases are made.

Fish are identified by both scientific and common names. Do not be put off by the scientific names of fish. The common names for many tropical fish vary from region to region and book to book. The only reliable way to identify fish, no matter where in the world you live, is by the scientific name given to each species.

Finally, as you read this book, set up your aquarium, and then select fish, I have one crucial piece of advice: Be patient. Take your time as trying to set up a tank too quickly can cause problems. Careful planning and thoughtful decisions will go a long way in helping make your aquarium a success.

AN OVERVIEW OF FISHKEEPING

1

AN OVERVIEW OF FISHKEEPING

People have been keeping fish in containers for more than a thousand years. Aquariums, as we know them, have been around for almost 150 years. The all-glass aquarium of today became available during the 1960s. A well-stocked aquarium or pet store will offer tanks ranging from a couple of gallons to a couple hundred gallons in capacity. Sophisticated filtration systems and a wide variety of equipment and accessories are available to help the aquarist in his or her hobby.

Despite all of this progress, one aspect of fishkeeping remains unchanged. An aquarium, no matter what size or shape, no matter how advanced the filter and lighting systems, is an *artificial* environment. It is a closed, self-contained system that bears almost no resemblance to a natural aquatic ecosystem. This concept may seem obvious, but many aquarists often lose sight of this fact.

Before reliable, efficient filtration systems were available, hobbyists would try to create a "balanced" aquarium, with the proper combination of fish, plants, and snails for the amount of water in the tank. Food and light would be controlled as much as possible to achieve the desired balance. By current standards, these tanks held very few fish. Nonetheless, even these tanks were vastly overcrowded in comparison with the natural world.

Observe any healthy natural aquatic ecosystem—be it stream or pond, river, or lake—and you will find that there are tens of thousands of gallons of water for each fish. If you could dip a 100-gallon (380-l) tank into a pond, for example, more often than not it would come up empty, which illustrates just how small even large aquariums are in comparison to the natural homes of fish.

Natural aquatic ecosystems also receive the benefit of seasonal or continual additions of clean, fresh water from streams, rain, or underground springs. In an aquarium, unless the hobbyist removes some water from the tank and replaces it with new water, the fish must live in the same water all of the time. Even with a good filtration system, the quality of aquarium water will deteriorate over time.

Obviously, closed aquatic systems can and do work, but not without attention to water quality. You will notice as you read this book that the theme of water quality is a common thread in many of the topics covered. The goal of the fishkeeper is to choose equipment, fish, and aquarium-management techniques that will maintain the best water quality possible.

Poor water quality creates physical stress for the fish, which is the primary cause of disease and death of aquarium fish. In this way fish are much like us. When under physical stress, the immune system is less able to deal with the disease-causing organisms that are always in the environment. With aquarium fish, as with humans, preventing disease is much easier than curing it.

Many novice hobbyists, unaware of the importance of water quality and its relation to disease, find themselves unable to keep fish alive for more than a few months. The fish mysteriously become ill and eventually die. When the hobbyist tires of replacing fish, the tank is emptied and then stored, sold, or given away. These unsuccessful fishkeepers are amazed when told that the fish they were unable to keep alive for more than six months should have lived for several years or more.

Many new hobbyists are disheartened to discover that fishkeeping is a combination of art and science. There may be more than one answer to the same question, depending on who you talk to or which book you read. The fact is, there is usually more than one way to set up a tank or solve a problem. The more you read and the more questions you ask, the better aquarist you will be. Every advanced hobbyist started out as a novice who was willing to learn about fishkeeping. Because there are so many variables from aquarium to aquarium and differences among the fish being kept, it sometimes becomes a matter of trial and error in discovering the optimal setup. Everyone makes mistakes; the important thing is to learn from them.

THE BIOLOGY OF AQUARIUMS

For fish, the water in an aquarium is their world. The chemical composition of the water and the substances dissolved in it have a significant effect on the health and well-being of the fish. Some species of fish are more adaptable than others to differences in water chemistry, and some species are more resistant to deteriorating water quality than others. This presents several challenges to the aquarist.

The chemical composition of tap water varies from one part of the country to another. It may be soft and acidic or hard and alkaline. The composition of the water where the fish live in nature also varies from region to region. The fish that live in locations where the water is consistent year-round have evolved and adapted to those conditions and do best when kept in aquarium water of similar composition. Fish native to areas where the water varies somewhat during the year due to heavy rainfall and flooding are more adaptable to a range of water conditions and are often easier to maintain in an aquarium.

There are no hard-and-fast rules regarding water composition. Most, if not all, of the fish available at your local aquarium or pet store should do fine in whatever kind of tap water you have. But there are exceptions. For example, if your water is very soft and acidic, fish that prefer water that is quite hard and alkaline will not be at their best. They may be less active, their colors will not be as intense, and they are very unlikely to breed. The same holds true for fish that prefer very soft, acidic water but are kept in rather hard, alkaline water. Some hobbyists are so keen for certain species of fish that they go to great effort to modify their tap water to the needs of the fish. The drawback in such a situation is that the hobbyist must keep a supply of the modified water available at all times for normal maintenance and for emergencies.

For aquarists who live in rural areas and have well water, there are other considerations. Some sources of well water have high levels of iron, copper, or other metals that can be toxic to fish over time. It may be necessary to have the water tested to determine if it contains compounds that are harmful to fish.

One problem that users of well water will not have is common to those who get their water from a municipal water company. Water departments usually treat the water they provide with chlorine or chloramine to kill harmful bacteria and certain kinds of algae that can give water an unpleasant taste. For fish, chlorine and chloramine can be deadly. You will find products at your local pet shop that are designed to remove or neutralize these chemicals. To determine which chemical has been added to your tap water, contact the water department. If chlorine is being used, a simple dechlorinator will do the job. However, if chloramine is being added to the water, it will be necessary to purchase a one-step water conditioner to deal with the problem. Chloramine is a combination of chlorine and ammonia. When a straight chlorine remover is added to the water in sufficient quantities, it will break the chemical bond between the chlorine and ammonia, removing the chlorine but releasing the ammonia. Ammonia, even in very small quantities, is extremely toxic to fish. A one-step water conditioner will remove the chlorine and then neutralize the ammonia.

Ammonia is also encountered in the biology of every aquatic environment. As soon as fish are added to an aquarium, ammonia begins to accumulate in the water. Some of this ammonia is a product of fish respiration and is released into the water through their gills. When the fish are fed, the resulting waste products from the fish also release ammonia into the water. Uneaten food in the tank also will be broken down to produce yet more ammonia. The increasing levels of this compound in the water represent a threat to the health of the fish.

Ammonia can actually appear in two forms, ammonia and ammonium, which is an ionic form of ammonia. The acidity or alkalinity of the water has a great effect on which form is more prevalent. The more acidic water is, the more ammonium is present, whereas the more alkaline water is, the greater the amount of ammonia. Of the two, it is ammonia that is toxic.

The acidity or alkalinity of water (or of anything else, for that matter) is measured as pH. The pH scale runs from 0 to 14, with 7.0 being neutral. Values below 7.0 are increasingly acid, whereas values above

Although an aquarium may appear to be a complete, natural aquatic system, it is, in fact, an artificial environment that requires careful planning and maintenance on the part of the aquarist.

Cylindrical tanks are a good choice for aquarists with space restrictions as they don't take up much room and provide fine fish viewing.

7.0 are increasingly alkaline. Because the pH scale is logarithmic, a change of one full unit is significant. For example, a change from 7.0 to 8.0 means that the water is ten times more alkaline. At pH 7.0, nontoxic ammonium is dominant, but as the pH increases, ammonia molecules become more numerous, making the problem of rising ammonia levels a significant danger.

Fortunately, nature has a way of dealing with ammonia known as the *nitrogen cycle.* The nitrogen cycle is central to every aspect of maintaining an aquarium, and understanding it is essential. The basic principles are very simple.

The nitrogen cycle requires the presence of nitrifying bacteria. A bacteria known as *Nitrosomonas* is able to convert the toxic nitrogen compound ammonia into another toxic nitrogen compound, nitrite. Another bacteria known as *Nitrobacter* is then able to convert nitrite to a much less toxic nitrogen compound, nitrate. That's it, except for the fact that it takes time for these bacteria to become available in sufficient numbers to handle the amounts of ammonia and nitrite in the water. These bacteria, by the way, are everywhere in our environment, not just in aquariums, and will find their way into the tank without your help.

In a new aquarium, it may take a few days, a week, or even longer for enough *Nitrosomonas* to become available to begin to convert the ammonia to nitrite. The more fish there are, the higher the initial ammonia levels will be. One potential problem resulting from this is that if ammonia levels are very high, the second type of bacteria, *Nitrobacter,* may be inhibited and will not begin to increase in numbers until the ammonia levels drop and the amount of nitrite begins to rise. This increases the amount of time the fish are exposed to high levels of ammonia.

On the other hand, if there are not enough fish to produce sufficiently high levels of ammonia, the *Nitrosomonas* may be unable to multiply faster than other types of bacteria that are also in the tank and the nitrogen cycle will not be completed properly. Once there are enough *Nitrosomonas,* the level of ammonia will peak and then begin to drop. At the same time, the levels of nitrite will begin to rise rapidly. Because it is as toxic as ammonia, nitrite can cause significant physical stress to fish. It will take weeks before there are enough *Nitrobacter* to control nitrite. Slowly, the level of nitrite will fall. After approximately six to eight weeks, the levels of both ammonia and nitrite will be insignificant. This initial process is known as breaking a tank in. The toxic effects of ammonia and nitrite on fish during this time have come to be known as "new tank syndrome."

Looking at the water in a tank gives no indication as to how the initial stages of the nitrogen cycle are progressing. The levels of ammonia and nitrite must be monitored using test kits, which will be described later in the book.

Experienced hobbyists have discovered that much of the stress caused to the fish by ammonia during the break-in period can be eliminated by adding a good-quality, one-step conditioner to the water. Apparently, the neutralized form of ammonia is still capable of feeding the *Nitrosomonas* bacteria. Some aquarists have found it even simpler to break in a tank by using household ammonia instead of fish. Enough ammonia must be added to register 10 milligrams per liter when testing the water with an ammonia test kit. It is important that the ammonia be unscented and contain no other additives or cleaning agents.

In an aquarium, the nitrogen cycle creates a sort of balance. As long as there are enough bacteria, ammonia and nitrite will be controlled. The bacteria will colonize every surface in the aquarium and in the filter. Clearly, the more surfaces there are, the more bacteria there can be. Because the gravel in a tank provides so much surface area, a special kind of filter, the undergravel filter, has become very popular among hobbyists. It will be discussed in detail in the section on filters.

You may be wondering about the end product of the nitrogen cycle, nitrate. Nitrate is relatively harmless to fish even at fairly high levels. As it accumulates in the water, it becomes food for plant life. If you have live plants in your tank, they will utilize the nitrate for food. If there are no live plants, or if there are live plants but the levels of nitrate are high enough, algae will consume the nitrate.

Algae is disliked by many new aquarists, who find it unattractive. But algae is part of all aquatic systems and is an indicator of their health. If a tank has sufficient illumination, green algae will grow on the surfaces in the tank. Insufficient light will result in brown algae. Tips on controlling algae can be found in the section on aquarium maintenance.

Do not be discouraged by what seems like a lot of information to remember. You will discover that much of what you learn comes from actually setting up and maintaining an aquarium. The information in this book is just to get you started.

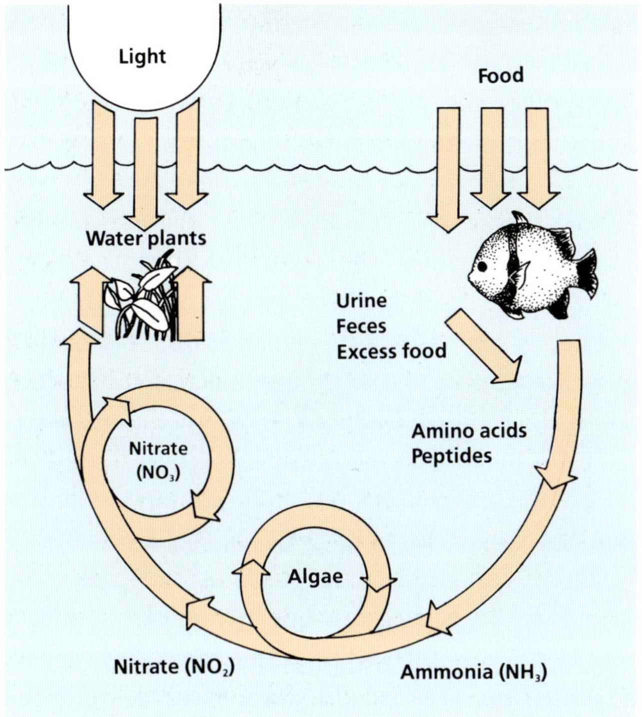

The nitrogen cycle is so essential to keeping fish healthy that it would be impossible to maintain an aquarium without it.

CHOOSING A DEALER

Before you purchase an aquarium or any equipment, and certainly before choosing fish, you should visit several aquarium or pet stores. The quality of the dealers who sell aquariums and fish varies considerably. Some store owners are only interested in having each customer spend as much money as possible. There is little concern about developing customer loyalty and satisfaction. At the opposite end of the spectrum are the shopkeepers who are hobbyists themselves and are interested in having customers who continue to patronize their stores.

A good dealer is a hobbyist's most valuable asset. The best stores provide more than just merchandise and fish. They also offer accurate information and help solve problems. There are a number of things to look for when visiting fish stores. Is the store clean? Is it well stocked? Do the fish appear active and healthy? Is there a good selection of books? Are the employees able to answer your questions? When they don't know the answer to a question, are they willing to find the answer for you?

Do not choose a dealer based on the price of the fish. Price, high or low, is not an indicator of quality. Do not expect a dealer to meet or beat the prices of discount mail-order companies. Keep in mind that the store owner must pay for the rent and lights, buy the equipment and supplies that are on the shelves, and pay the salaries of the employees. Remember, you want service and quality, good advice, and someone who is genuinely interested in your success as a hobbyist.

SELECTING AN AQUARIUM

Every year, tens of thousands of 10-gallon (38-l) starter kits are sold. This is usually the new hobbyist's first mistake. Although a 10-gallon (38-l) tank seems like it holds a lot of water, it really doesn't. The starter kit supposedly comes with everything you need to

The best way to choose an aquarium is to first determine the types and numbers of fish you wish to keep, then select the size and shape of tank that will properly house them.

set up the tank except fish. In truth, the equipment and accessories are generally inexpensive and of poor quality. Gravel and plants are often not included. The price may be attractive, but stay away from prepackaged setups; choosing an aquarium is a little more complicated than that.

There are several approaches. First, however, you should decide how much money you feel comfortable spending to set up an aquarium. Although the aquarium hobby is less expensive than many others, you will discover that the total cost of a new setup is probably more than you expect.

The best method for deciding on an aquarium, but one seldom practiced, is to first choose the fish you want to keep. Your dealer will be able to tell you, based on the number of fish you want and the sizes they will grow to, what size tank you will need. Despite the obvious good sense of this approach, only experienced hobbyists use it regularly.

Another approach—one you will need to consider even if you initially select a tank based on your choice of fish—is to determine where the tank is going to be in your home. It is very important to take into account the size and weight of the tank. Once an aquarium is set up, it will weigh approximately 10 pounds per gallon (5 kg per l). This means that you could be dealing with a minimum of 100 pounds (45 kg) or, more likely, 200 to 300 pounds (90 to 136 kg). If you choose a large display tank, let's say 55 gallons (209 l), its weight will exceed 500 pounds (225 kg).

What are you going to set the tank on? Delicate end tables with elegant finishes are unlikely to hold a few hundred pounds reliably. Shelves, whether in bookcases or attached to walls, may bend under the weight of even 100 pounds (45 kg). It is almost always best to purchase a stand with the aquarium. The nicest ones have shelves for supplies and doors to hide filters and equipment.

The tank must be in a location that will be convenient for regular aquarium maintenance. This is no small matter. If the tank is hard to get to or work around, you will end up putting off normal maintenance. As a result, the water quality and the appearance of the aquarium will begin to deteriorate. You should also keep in mind that no matter how careful you are, sooner or later water will be spilled and splashed outside the tank. Do not place the tank near valuable furniture, books, or anything else that you don't want to get wet.

The floor where the tank will sit should be as level as possible. If it is not, the water line at the top of the tank will be higher at one end than the other. An uneven load on the tank may also result in leaks. The weight of the tank should be distributed evenly on the floor. If a large amount of weight is transmitted to the floor at only the four points where the legs meet the floor, the actual load in pounds per square inch can be very high, enough to go through or severely dent wood floors. It may be necessary to place the stand on lengths of wood that will distribute the weight over a larger area.

As for environmental considerations, do not place the aquarium near a window or door. Direct sunlight can overheat a tank and also cause significant algae problems. Open doorways can be a source of drafts.

Place your aquarium where the fish are easy to view and the tank is easy to maintain. If normal tank maintenance, such as regular partial water changes and filter cleaning, is difficult, such tasks will tend to be put off and the water quality will deteriorate.

In short, you want to place the tank where you can control the temperature and light.

Taking into account available space and money, you should purchase the largest tank you can. There are several reasons for this. First and foremost, the more water a tank can hold, the more stable it will be as an aquatic environment. A larger tank will also allow you to keep more and larger fish—within limits, of course (stocking levels are discussed below). In addition, a larger tank makes it easier to keep fish that

When stocking an aquarium, you should consider the adult size of the fish you select to determine how many fish can be added to the tank.

need more room in which to live because of personality or behavior. This is an important but often overlooked point. Some fish are more territorial than others and will take over much of a smaller tank, leaving the rest of the inhabitants to share what remains. Some fish are more active and will nip any convenient fin that is nearby. A larger tank gives each fish more places to hide in peace and quiet.

New hobbyists, no matter how well intentioned, usually manage to overstock their first aquariums. The reason is simple. The initial assumption is that overcrowding means running out of room in the tank. To the inexperienced aquarist, empty space indicates that there is still room for a few more fish. Unfortunately, even after finding out that a tank can be overstocked long before the tank looks full, the aquarist has little to go by for guidance.

A typical rule of thumb—and there are several—is based on the size of the fish in inches. Thus "One inch of fish per gallon of water" (2.5 cm of fish per 3.8 l of water) is a commonly repeated guideline. This rule, however, is of no practical value. Some fish are slim, whereas others are deep-bodied and have more mass per inch of length. The amounts of oxygen required and waste products produced increase as the mass of the fish goes up. In addition, aquariums do not always hold as much water as they are labeled for. This is not a matter of consumer fraud. The gallonage listed on the label of the tank may be rounded up or down by a gallon or two, depending on the dimensions of the tank, to simplify the listing and pricing of aquariums. Although not a problem with lightly stocked tanks, the lack of a few gallons of water could be more serious if the tank is stocked to capacity. It is also important to remember that gravel, rocks, and other aquascaping items in an aquarium will reduce the volume of water it contains. A 45-gallon (170-l) tank may hold less than 40 gallons (152 l) after it is set up.

Gallons are not the only measurement with which aquarists have to be concerned. The surface area of a tank is just as important. In other words, you also have to know the amount of water surface (and gravel surface) available as a result of the dimensions of the aquarium. Along the surface of the water oxygen is acquired and carbon dioxide is released. For fish, as for people, the levels of oxygen and carbon dioxide determine how healthy an environment is. As you will learn in the discussion on filters later in this book, the undergravel filter, which functions as the biological filter for the tank, can support more nitrifying bacteria when more gravel surface area is available.

To deal with surface area instead of gallonage, another rule of thumb states that an aquarium should have "One inch of fish for every 24 square inches of surface area" (2.5 cm of fish for every 155 square cm of surface area). This guideline doesn't take into account the individual physical qualities of fish, the same shortcoming of the inch-per-gallon rule noted above, although it does take into account the actual amount of surface area available.

Walking into a well-stocked pet store and asking for a 20-gallon (76-l) aquarium is not as simple as it seems. You may be offered a regular 20, a "long" 20, and a "show" 20. They may all hold 20 gallons (76 l) of water, but they will have different amounts of surface area because of their different dimensions. For example, a show tank has more front glass-viewing area because it is taller than a regular 20-gallon (76-l) tank; it is also narrower front to back, has less surface area, and holds fewer fish.

By increasing the amount of filtration and frequency of aquarium maintenance, it is possible to keep larger numbers of fish in a tank than gallonage and surface area measurements ordinarily dictate, but this doesn't take into account all of the things that can go wrong, such as power outages and equipment failures. Therefore, in addition to buying the largest tank you can in terms of volume, choose the one that has the most surface area for its volume.

FILTRATION

As soon as fish are added to a newly set up aquarium, the water quality begins to deteriorate. This is the nature of a closed-system aquatic environment. Filtration systems are designed to maintain good water quality under these conditions. The purpose of filtration is not really to increase the number of fish that may be safely kept in a tank, although it can do this. The goal is to maintain the quality of the water for a moderately stocked tank with a margin of safety. For all practical purposes, every problem in an aquarium can be traced back to poor water quality. By combining sensible stocking levels with effective filtration and good aquarium management techniques, fishkeeping is essentially trouble free.

There are three kinds of filtration required: *mechanical, chemical,* and *biological.* In very lightly stocked tanks, one filter may do all three jobs. Most aquarists, however, generally want more fish in their tanks, which means using at least two kinds of filters in the filtration system to provide enough filtering capacity.

Mechanical filtration is designed to remove bits and pieces of solid material from the water. For many

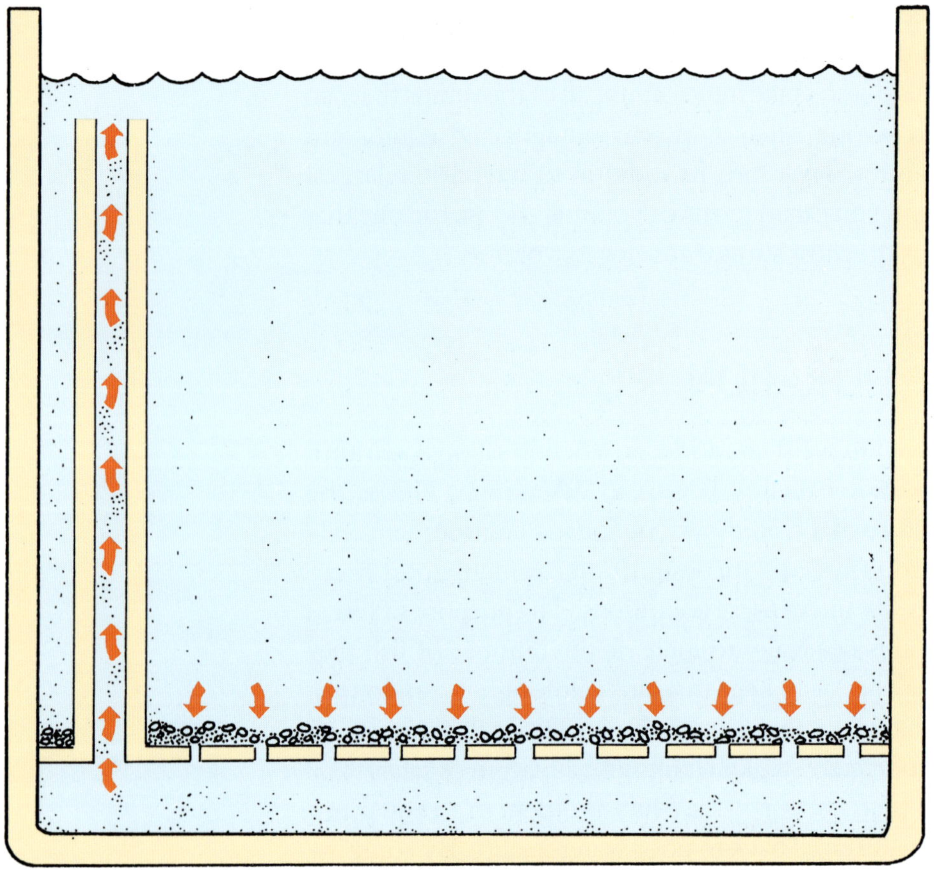

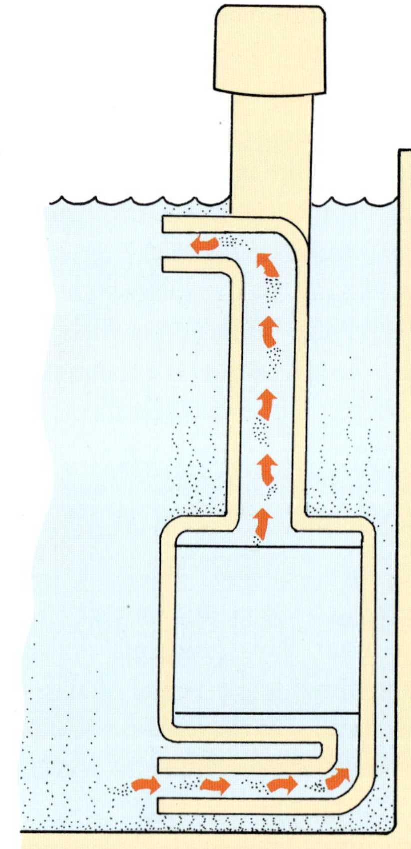

These are typical examples of three types of filters. **Left to right:** undergravel filter, internal power filter, external power filter.

new hobbyists, this is what the term filtration means. They assume that if there isn't any "junk" floating around in the water, the water must be clean. Although this assumption is not actually true, mechanical filtration is important. The process is simple: Water passes through a material that catches and holds the bits and pieces of solid matter.

The simplest device for this kind of filtration is the inside box or corner filter. Air from a small pump is used to pull water through the box. Although inexpensive, these filters are not particularly efficient and certainly add nothing to the beauty of the tank. Air-powered filters that were developed to hang on the back of the tank overcome the aesthetic problem of the inside filter but are no more efficient. These items have faded from the hobby and are now seldom seen.

Today, outside power filters are used to remove solid matter from the water. There are two kinds of power filters. One design hangs on the back of the tank, whereas the other design, known as a canister

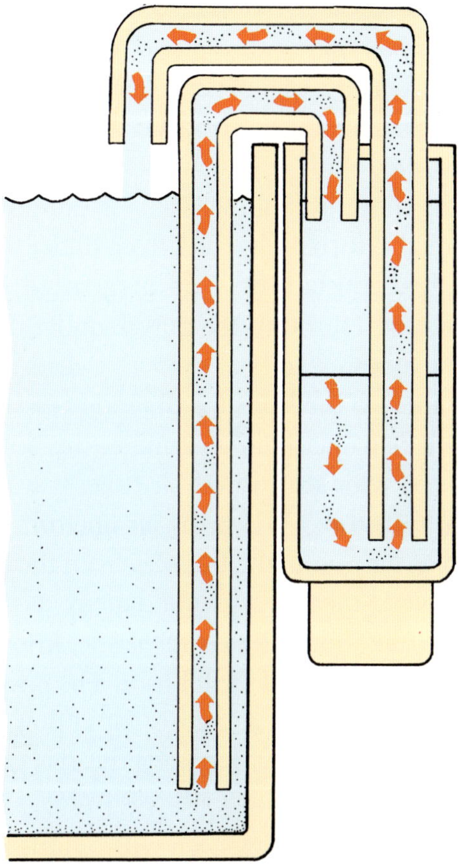

filter, can be placed on a shelf or the floor. These filters use quiet, reliable electric motors to pump water through the filtering material. The size of the filter required is determined by the capacity of the tank. The filter should be large enough to circulate the tank volume four or five times per hour. Thus a 40-gallon (152-l) aquarium would need a filter rated at 200 gallons (760 l) per hour. Keep in mind that filters are rated for flow when empty. Filtering material will reduce the flow by about a third.

The size of particles removed from the water will depend on the filtering material being used. There are trade-offs here. A material that filters very fine particles might appear to be the most desirable, but because it will clog much more rapidly, the filter will have to be cleaned more often. Cleaning a power filter, while not particularly difficult or time-consuming, is not a task that most aquarists want to face every week or so. Normal filter maintenance should be required only once each month or every other month. (Canister filters are somewhat harder to clean than those that hang on the back of the tank.)

Chemical filtration can also be accomplished with a power filter. Even though the water may look clean after mechanical filtration, there are numerous dissolved waste products still in the water. Along with the mechanical filtering material, there is room in the power filter for a chemical filtering material. Although there are several types of products on the market to do this job, the best material to use is good-quality granular activated carbon (GAC). GAC should not be confused with charcoal, which is sometimes sold in pet stores but is far less effective than carbon.

GAC is very effective at removing dissolved waste products from the water, but only if the water actually passes over it. Some power filters use special cartridges of GAC, but these cartridges have two faults. First, they seldom hold enough GAC; within a week or two the GAC is saturated and ceases to remove waste products. Second, the cartridges seldom fit into the filter tightly enough. A rule of physics is that water takes the route of least resistance. Thus, if the cartridge does not fit tightly enough, the water simply goes around it and never comes into contact with the GAC.

Approximately 1 ounce (28 g) of GAC should be used for every 4 gallons (15 l) of water. If a cartridge does not hold that much, or if it fits too loosely, open it up and add more GAC. When used in sufficient quantities in a typical aquarium, the GAC will need to be changed every four to eight weeks. One way of determining if the GAC needs to be changed is to hold a sheet of white paper behind the tank. If the paper looks yellowish when viewed through the tank, the GAC needs to be replaced. It is important that water passes through the mechanical filtration material before it reaches the GAC. If the surfaces of the GAC become coated with solid waste products, chemical filtration will not occur.

To a certain degree, the mechanical filtering material and the GAC also serve as biological filters because nitrifying bacteria will colonize these areas of the power filter. Unfortunately, every time the filter medium and GAC are changed, the bacteria are also removed. Some power filters contain an area that is filled with ceramic noodles or rings, which provide surfaces for the nitrifying bacteria. These ceramic pieces can be lightly rinsed off, but are never cleaned or disposed of. If there are not many fish in the tank, these ceramic pieces can provide sufficient biological filtration.

In a very lightly stocked tank, there are sufficient numbers of bacteria on the gravel and other surfaces to provide adequate biological filtration. For a normally stocked tank, however, the best way to ensure effective biological filtration is to use an undergravel filter in conjunction with a power filter. An undergravel filter consists of a plastic plate with numerous slots in it that sits on the bottom of the tank. This plate is covered with gravel. At the back of the plate are one or more lift tubes. Water is drawn up the tubes, which in turn pulls water from under the plate. As a result, a constant flow of oxygenated water is circulated down through the gravel, under the plate, and up the tubes.

There are two methods for drawing water up the tubes. One is to place an airstone at the bottom of each tube. (A wide selection of airstones is available at any aquarium store.) When the air line tube is connected to an air pump, the bubbles from the airstone lift the water up the tube. A second method is to place a small electric motor sealed in plastic, known as a powerhead, at the top of the lift tube. The powerhead pulls water up the tube at a fairly rapid flow rate. In fact, on small tanks only one powerhead is generally needed.

Studies have shown that even with as little as 1 inch (2.54 cm) of gravel, an undergravel filter is so efficient that there is more than enough biological filtration regardless of the number of fish. This efficiency, however, can be reduced if the gravel becomes clogged with solid matter. By using a power filter, many of these particles can be removed from the water before they enter the gravel. Some undergravel filters come with disposable cartridges of GAC that are supposed to be placed at the top of the lift tubes. These should be discarded. The cartridges significantly restrict the flow of water up the lift tubes, and they contain so little GAC that they would have to be replaced two or three times per week. The power filter can provide far more efficient and effective chemical filtration.

Even with the use of a power filter, gravel eventually accumulates quite a bit of solid matter. The best way to deal with this is by using a gravel "vacuum." A gravel vacuum consists of a long hose with a large plastic tube at one end that is pushed into the gravel. As water is siphoned out of the tank, the gravel is swirled around in the tube, releasing any solids. The dirty water is siphoned out, but the gravel remains in the aquarium. Many hobbyists use a gravel vacuum when doing periodic water changes.

AERATION

Fish are able to breathe in water by removing dissolved oxygen from the water with their gills and releasing carbon dioxide in exchange. Nitrifying bacteria also use oxygen to metabolize ammonia and nitrite. Dissolved oxygen is introduced to aquarium water at the surface, where carbon dioxide is also released into the atmosphere. In order to ensure that sufficient oxygen is dissolved in the water, from the bottom of the tank to the top, aeration must be used.

If an undergravel filter is in place, the rising air bubbles will circulate the water in the tank and also agitate the surface of the water. Contrary to popular belief, the air bubbles themselves do not contribute any significant amounts of oxygen to the water. The importance of air bubbles is that they disturb the surface of the water, thereby increasing the exchange of oxygen and carbon dioxide.

Unless a power filter or powerhead has a special aeration attachment, it will not provide the necessary aeration. In such cases, the best solution is one or more airstones powered by an air pump. The bubbles from the stones will circulate the water and create turbulence at the surface.

LIGHTING

A cover and light for a tank do more than make the aquarium look attractive. The cover keeps dust out, reduces water evaporation, and prevents fish from jumping out while preventing animals and the hands of children from getting in. Lights provide controlled illumination.

Most aquariums are supplied with hoods equipped with one or two sockets for incandescent light bulbs. If you are not going to maintain live plants and the fish that you choose prefer subdued lighting, regular light bulbs may be fine. The typical bulb for an aquarium hood is long rather than round, to provide more even illumination, and will be rated at 15 or 25 watts. Light bulbs have two disadvantages: They generate enough heat to raise the temperature of the water in smaller tanks, and they cost more to run than fluorescent tubes.

The initial cost of fluorescent tubes is higher than light bulbs. A kit to convert the tank hood from incandescent to fluorescent lighting is required, and the tubes are more expensive than light bulbs. In the long run, however, fluorescents have several advantages. They do not generate as much heat per watt as normal bulbs, they provide much more even lighting, and they cost far less to operate.

If you are going to grow aquatic plants, fluorescent lighting is a necessity. Generally, two tubes are required to provide sufficient light. Choose tubes that are specifically designed for growing plants. A rule of thumb is to provide 3 watts of lighting per gallon of water. The duration of lighting is also important. Because there are so many variables—such as the number of fish, the types of plants, and the water quality—it is best to start with ten hours of light each day and see how things go. If there is too much light, green algae will become quite evident. Insufficient light will result in poor plant growth and perhaps some brown algae. By using a timer to turn the lights off and on, it is possible to adjust the number of hours per day until you obtain the best overall results; the timer ensures that the same number of hours of light is provided each day.

HEATERS

Maintaining the correct water temperature is essential to the health of the fish. The term *tropical fish* refers to species that prefer temperatures between 74° and 84°F (23° and 29°C). The temperature of the water should also be relatively stable. It should not vary more than a few degrees over a period of twenty-four hours. To achieve these goals, it is necessary to purchase a good-quality heater. Do not try to save money on this item. Inexpensive heaters will cause problems. The thermostat, which maintains the temperature, is seldom reliable in an inexpensive heater.

Should the thermostat stick in the closed position, the heater will stay on, raising the water temperature to lethal levels. If the thermostat sticks in the open position, the water temperature will fall to that of the room the tank is in. During the warmer months of the year, this may not be as much of a problem as it can be with colder weather. Rapidly rising or falling temperatures are worse for the fish than more moderate rates of change.

Small aquariums, which contain less water and therefore have less mass, are much more susceptible to rapid changes in water temperature. It will take longer for a malfunctioning heater to cause the water in a large tank to rise or fall to dangerous levels. This will give an aquarist adequate time to detect the problem, assuming, of course, that the temperature of the tank is checked every day or two.

Heaters are rated by wattage. The usual recommendation for selecting the correct size heater is 5 watts per gallon of water, but you may wish to choose a less powerful heater instead, say 3 watts per gallon. At 5 watts per gallon, the heater will raise the temperature of 1 gallon (3.8 l) of water by 1 degree Fahrenheit in one hour. Thus, a 15-gallon (57-l) tank would require a 75-watt heater. Do not buy a heater of higher wattage than necessary for the size tank you have. Should the thermostat stick in the closed position, a larger heater will raise the water temperature so quickly you may not have time to notice it. As it is, even at the recommended wattage per gallon, there

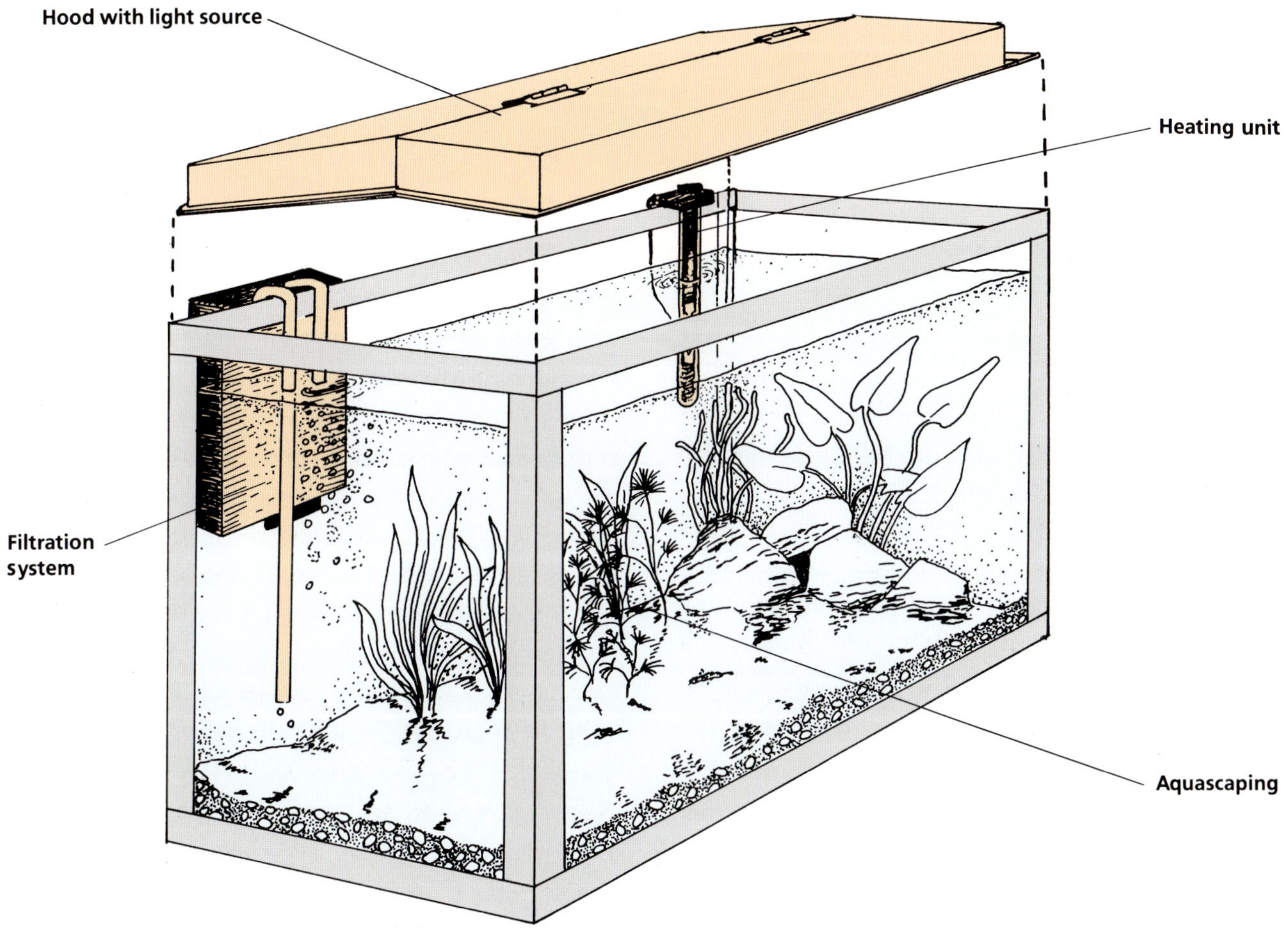

Aquarium setups do not have to be complex. A filter, heater, and a hood with light are all that are necessary, along with gravel and plants to aquascape the tank.

can be problems with smaller tanks. In a 15-gallon (57-l) aquarium, for example, a sticking heater will raise the water temperature to well above 90°F (32°C) in less than twenty-four hours. Should you fail to notice the rising temperature during this period, the fish are not likely to survive. Some hobbyists minimize the likelihood of this problem by using 3 watts per gallon as a guideline when choosing a heater. For a 15-gallon (57-l) tank, this would mean a 50-watt heater. The 50-watt heater will maintain the

15-gallon (57-l) tank at the same temperature as the 75-watt heater, but it will take about twice as long to raise water temperatures, thus giving you more time to notice any problems.

TEST KITS

Even though every pet and aquarium store stocks test kits, surprisingly few hobbyists purchase them. Test kits are not expensive or difficult to use, and they are the only way to actually measure the quality of the water. Every aquarist should have kits to measure ammonia, nitrite, and pH. There are many other kinds of kits available as well, including kits to measure nitrate, copper, dissolved oxygen, chlorine, and so on.

When a tank is being broken in, test kits can be used to monitor the nitrogen cycle. After that, the kits can be used on a periodic basis to make sure that ammonia and nitrite remain unmeasurable and that the pH is stable. If any of the fish should become ill, your first response should be to check the water quality for problems that could be creating stress for the fish.

Test kits have either liquid or dry reagents to process the water being tested. Dry reagents are preferable because they have a longer shelf life and will give more reliable results. It is also helpful to note that the better kits also are dated to indicate how long the reagents will remain effective.

AQUASCAPING

Decorating an aquarium is largely a matter of personal taste. This does not mean, however, that iridescent gravel and fluorescent orange plants should be used. Choose natural or darker-colored gravel for the tank. The fish will look their best when the gravel is relatively subdued in brightness and color. Gravel size is important also, particularly if the tank is equipped with an undergravel filter. If the pieces of gravel are too large, there will be less surface area for the nitrifying bacteria to colonize and small bits of solid matter will pass through the gravel easily and remain in suspension. If the gravel size is too small, the gravel bed will clog rather quickly because of the tiny spaces between the grains of gravel. Number 2 or number 3 gravel, which are approximately 2 or 3 millimeters in diameters respectively, are good sizes.

Although studies have indicated that only an inch of gravel is required for an undergravel filter to provide sufficient biological filtration, a layer that is somewhat deeper will be needed to provide enough depth for plants to root or to conceal the bases of artificial plants. There should be more gravel at the back of the tank, so that the gravel bed slopes downward toward the front. There are three reasons why this is preferable. First, in order to ensure that water is drawn through the gravel bed and the undergravel filter evenly, the water must travel through the gravel nearest the lift tubes more slowly so that the water farthest away from the tubes is also drawn through the gravel bed. The easiest way to ensure this is by having a thicker layer of gravel nearest the lift tubes to slow the flow of water. Second, if the gravel slopes downward toward the front, accumulated wastes will tend to end up nearer the front of the tank, making it easier to siphon this material out. Third, when an aquarium is filled with water, an optical phenomenon makes the tank look narrower than it really is. The sloping gravel counters this effect, making the aquarium look somewhat deeper front to back.

The varieties of plants you choose, whether plastic or live, are up to you. Some hobbyists determine which plants are normally found where the fish in the tank originate and use only those species. Although this is a nice touch, it is not really necessary and makes sense only if all the fish in the tank are from the same region or locality.

When mixing live plants in a tank, keep in mind that if they are from different parts of the world, they will probably have different requirements for water chemistry, temperature, and light. Although usually adaptable to a range of conditions, it is best to purchase plants that have relatively similar needs. Some types of plants, particularly those with fine or delicate leaves, are more likely to be eaten by fish that prefer vegetable matter than are plants with larger, thicker leaves.

When choosing rocks for a tank, avoid those that will alter the chemistry of the water. Corals and sea shells not only look inappropriate in a freshwater tank but can also make the water much harder and more alkaline. If you are keeping fish that do best in hard, alkaline water and are having a difficult time maintaining these conditions, the best solution is to add one part crushed oyster shells to five parts aquarium gravel. Rocks with rough surfaces and sharp edges can cause accidental injuries to fish that are used to living around rocks with smooth surfaces.

Many of the "unusual" aquariums are designed for people, not fish, and should be avoided.

One of your goals in aquascaping is to provide sufficient hiding places for the fish. Fish that are active at night will seek daytime shelter. If denied hiding places, they will be nervous and insecure. Some species, desperate for shelter, will hide behind the aquarium heater and may suffer severe and even fatal burns. Fish also seek shelter when being chased or harassed by other fish in the tank. By using rocks, you can create caves, nooks, and crannies for the fish. Just make sure that the rockwork is secure. Otherwise, it may fall, cracking the glass of the tank. If you keep species of fish that like to dig, rockwork should rest on the bottom of the tank, not on the surface of the gravel.

Driftwood can look very attractive in an aquarium, and some species of suckermouth catfish from South America appear to gnaw on driftwood to

The territorial and breeding behaviors of fish are so interesting that hobbyists often set up additional tanks to house new species.

obtain some nutritional benefit. It is important that the driftwood be cured so that it contains no toxic or harmful chemicals that could leach into the water and endanger the health of the fish. Even properly cured driftwood will leach acidic tannins and lignins into the water that will tint the water a yellow or reddish brown color. Although this will not harm the fish, and may actually make the water chemistry more suitable for fish that prefer acidic water, some aquarists object to the appearance of the water. Because driftwood is an organic material, it will slowly decay and over time may become a source of difficulty in maintaining good water quality. Frequent partial water changes are even more important if you keep driftwood in your aquarium.

Above all else, avoid placing treasure chests, sunken ships, or any of the other even more ghastly items that are available, in your tank. An aquarium may not be a natural ecosystem, but it can look as natural as possible if aquascaped with suitable materials.

If you don't want your aquatic decor to be undone, choose the fish for your aquarium with care. Some species are prone to moving gravel and undermining rocks and can completely destroy all of your efforts in a few days.

FEEDING

Choosing the correct foods and learning how to feed aquarium fish can often mean the difference between success and failure in fishkeeping. No matter how good the water quality, fish cannot grow to adulthood and remain healthy without a balanced diet and proper nutrition. The amount and frequency of feedings are also important.

In nature, fish have adapted to the food resources that are available at different times of the year. Feeding habits evolved to cope with the need to eat while remaining safe from predators. Consequently, the aquarist must be prepared to provide the necessary foods while taking into account the differences in how various species go about the business of feeding.

The most common mistake that new hobbyists make is to feed too much. Overfeeding results in large amounts of decaying food in the tank, quickly leading to significant water quality problems. It is essential to keep in mind that a fish has a proportionally small stomach for its size. The general recommendation is to feed the quantity of food that the fish can consume in five minutes.

In natural settings, fish eat small amounts of food all day long; hunting for food is a continual activity. For this reason, it is always better to feed several small meals per day, not one large one.

No matter how well-balanced and nutritious the diet you provide may be, it will be of little value if the food doesn't reach the fish it is intended for. In the typical community aquarium, some fish are more aggressive than others. They swim faster and eat faster. Those species that move more slowly and pick leisurely at their food will never get enough to eat because they cannot compete for food successfully against their quicker tankmates. The obvious solution is to avoid combining species of fish that have very dissimilar feeding habits. An alternative is to feed the more aggressive fish until they are full and then offer additional food to the quieter species.

This feeding regimen also applies when bottom-feeding fish are in the tank. In order to make sure that sufficient food reaches the bottom without overfeeding, the fish that swim higher up in the tank must be fed first.

Many bottom-dwelling fish, particularly catfish, prefer to feed at night. In the wild, this strategy helps them avoid predators. To satisfy the needs of these fish, they must be fed just before turning off the tank lights in the evening. The fish that are active during the day will not feed in the darkness.

A glance at the shelves of food in any well-stocked aquarium or pet store reveals a wide variety of choices. The nutritional balance of proteins, carbohydrates, fats, minerals, and other components varies according to the kinds of fish being fed. Commer-

This suckermouth catfish is a nocturnal species that requires a lot of vegetable matter in its diet.

cially prepared foods are offered in several forms: flakes, pellets, and freeze-dried. In addition, frozen foods are usually available. As with human beings, fish are much more likely to receive a balanced diet when several different kinds of foods are provided. Except for very specialized feeders, most fish will readily accept prepared foods.

When shopping for foods, you should purchase them from a store that does a large volume of business. Fish foods have a limited shelf life, even when packaged in sealed containers, so it is best to buy them where the stock turnover is high. Do not purchase large sizes unless you have a lot of fish to feed. Once opened, the nutritional value of the food deteriorates rather quickly. Within six months, the food remaining in an opened container is estimated to lose more than half its nutritional value.

To provide a *very* well-balanced diet, feed your fish live food occasionally. (Fish also seem to enjoy hunting for live food, such as brine shrimp, in their tank.) Many dealers offer live foods, which may vary in availability depending on the season and the weather. Frozen foods also offer good nutritional value.

SETTING UP THE TANK

Before beginning the process of setting up an aquarium, make sure you have all the equipment you will need to complete the project, except for the fish. The tank should be up and running for at least a day before you even think about adding fish. Take your time and follow these instructions closely.

Make absolutely sure that the tank is where you want it to be. Once you add water, the tank cannot be moved without first emptying it. The tank will be much too heavy to move when full, and if moved when partially filled with water, the uneven load could stress the aquarium, creating leaks. You should have several towels available to deal with any spills that will occur.

If you are going to cover the back of the aquarium with colored foil, crystalizing paint, or an aquatic scene background, now is the time to do so. Once the background material is installed, the tank can be set in place. Wipe the interior of the tank with a damp rag.

If you are using an undergravel filter, it should now be assembled and placed in the tank. For large aquariums, there are usually two filter plates, but smaller tanks will have only one. If the plate is a little narrower front to back than the tank, place it against the back of the tank. Install the lift tubes and you are ready to add the gravel.

You should have approximately two pounds of gravel for every gallon (.9 kg of gravel for every liter) of water. Place some of the gravel in a bucket and rinse it very thoroughly. Dump the rinsed gravel into the tank and continue the process until all of the gravel has been washed and placed in the aquarium. Do not use soap or any other cleaning material, just plain water.

The gravel should be arranged so that it slopes gently toward the front of the tank. If you want to create a terrace or two, use small stones or rocks to build a retaining wall and add additional gravel to form the terrace. Add any additional rocks and other aquascaping materials, but do not add plants now. The aquarium heater can be installed, but it should not be plugged in until it is submerged up to the waterline mark, usually indicated on the body of the heater. This is also a good time to place the thermometer in the tank. Thermometers designed to attach to the outside of the glass can also be used.

Place some newspapers or a small bowl or plate on the gravel. The idea is to break the stream of water as it is added to the tank to prevent disturbing the gravel. Using a bucket, add cold water to the tank until it is approximately one-half to two-thirds full. Warm or hot water may crack the glass. Remove the newspapers or dish and step back to look at what you have accomplished thus far.

With careful planning, aquariums can be designed into the decor of any room.

You will notice that the back of the tank appears closer to the front than it did when it was empty. Rocks that seemed nicely spaced now may appear to be too close together. Move then until you are satisfied and then begin adding the plants. Take your time. Because you will be looking down into the tank when placing the plants in the gravel, you will need to step back and observe the results from the front of the tank. Rearrange the plants as much as necessary until you are satisfied with the overall look of the aquarium.

Finish filling the tank, being careful not to disturb the aquascaping. An easy way to do this is to place an open hand, palm up, just below the surface of the water and pour the water onto your hand, thereby

Healthy aquarium fish will easily live three years or more.

dispersing the flow away from the bottom of the tank and the aquascaping.

Plug the heater in and adjust it until the light that indicates it is working comes on. It will take some time for the heater to raise the temperature of the water. When the light goes out, indicating that the thermostat in the heater has opened and switched the heater off, check the temperature. If it is still too low, adjust the heater until the light comes on again. Follow this procedure until the water temperature is where it should be. A good temperature for most tropical fish is 76° to 78°F (23° to 25°C).

Attach air line tubing from the air pump to the airstones in the lift tubes of the undergravel filter. Plug in the pump and adjust the flow of the air valves until the air bubbles in the tubes look even in quantity. If you are using powerheads instead, place them at the top of the lift tubes, plug them in, and adjust the rate of flow. If the powerheads do not agitate the surface of the water enough, you should add an air pump and airstones to the tank as well.

If you are going to use an outside power filter, assemble it per the manufacturer's instructions and hook it up. If everything appears to be operating correctly, add a good-quality water conditioner to remove any chlorine or chloramine. Then, cover the tank and turn on the light. Clean the outside glass and admire your new aquarium.

Resist the temptation to go shopping for fish. You want the tank to operate for at least twenty-four hours so that the temperature stabilizes and you are sure that all of the equipment is working as it should. Instead of shopping for fish, read about them. The more you know before you begin the selection process, the better off you will be.

DISEASE

Nothing is more discouraging to a new hobbyist than dead and dying fish. Fish diseases seem mysterious to many aquarists, and many ex-hobbyists are convinced that fish are fragile, sickly creatures. Entire books have been written on the subject of fish disease, and new ones are published on a regular basis. Put simply, diagnosing and treating fish diseases is complicated.

The fact is, however, that given good aquarium conditions, fish are quite capable of remaining healthy. Their immune systems are as well developed as those of humans. But, the stress caused by poor water quality will significantly reduce the effectiveness of these immune systems. Remember, preventing disease is always easier than trying to cure it.

Perhaps the most important thing you can do is observe your fish closely. Learn how they normally act. The first clue to problems is when the fish behave abnormally or look different than usual. Perhaps they have changed color, are swimming in a different part of the tank, or their fins are clamped together. If any of the fish appear to be distressed in some way, immediately test the water, looking for elevated nitrite levels or pH that is too low. If the water quality is not as good as it should be, change 50 percent of the water and then try to determine if the source of the problem is in the filter system.

DO NOT place any medications in the tank. Using medications is always the *last* step in the process, not the first. The aquarium medication industry is largely unregulated by the government. Most, but not all, aquarium medications are vastly underdosed as packaged, and many are ineffective against common aquarium diseases. Be very careful of antibiotics. Studies have shown that some, such as erythromycin, are only effective against typical aquarium diseases at doses so high that the nitrifying bacteria in the biological filter are killed, worsening the problem.

More often than not, it is the accompanying water changes recommended on the packages of many medications, not the drugs, that cure the problem. In fact, the fishes' immune system is often responsible for recovery from disease, simply as a result of improved environmental conditions in the aquarium.

Because the topic of fish disease is so large, there is not enough space to adequately deal with the subject here. It is best to refer to specialized books, which are available from better pet and aquarium stores.

The one disease I will discuss here is probably the most common one and the easiest to cure. It is called white-spot disease but is most commonly known by the term *ich,* which comes from the name of the parasite that causes it, *Ichthyophthirius multifillis*. This parasite is always in the aquarium environment, but the immune systems of the fish are more than capable of dealing with it as long as aquarium conditions are good. It is only when the fish are under physical stress that the immune response is depressed and the parasite can take hold.

The parasite is tiny and cannot be seen until it attaches to the fish and forms a cyst, a tiny white spot that is visible on the fish. Once mature, the parasite falls to the bottom of the tank and within a day releases up to a thousand free-swimming newborn parasites. These young parasites must find a host fish within two days or they will die; it is during this phase of the life cycle of the parasite that it is vulnerable to being killed by medications.

The higher the temperature of the water, the faster the life cycle is. Some hobbyists have cured fish of *ich* by raising the water temperature to about 84°F (29°C) and changing 50 percent of the water every day. The more practical and effective solution for most aquarists is to raise the water temperature and treat the tank with a combination of malachite green and formalin, used according to the directions on the bottle. This is the most effective medication for dealing with outbreaks of *ich.* It is essential, however, that any carbon in the filter system be removed during treatment. Otherwise, the carbon will absorb the medication from the water.

CHOOSING FISH

Walk into a large aquarium store and you may be confronted with three or four hundred tanks with hundreds of species of fish. The choices can be overwhelming. Obviously, a 15- or 20-gallon (57- or 76-l) tank—even a 50-gallon (190-l) tank—will hold only a small selection of the fish that are available. Most hobbyists start out by keeping a community tank because it contains fish of different shapes and colors, creating a varied and interesting display.

In a way, choosing a good combination of fish is actually harder than setting up a tank because there are so many variables. It is essential that the species selected be compatible, but compatibility represents a number of factors. Reading about the characteristics and care of different species of fish can help you decide what types might be good choices. A knowledgeable dealer can also answer your questions concerning the best fish for your first community tank.

Let's start by examining some basic principles to keep in mind. To begin with, dealers' tanks are vastly overstocked. The fish are in these aquariums only a short time, and store personnel perform extensive maintenance on the tanks to keep water quality very good. Your aquarium at home should never be stocked to this density. In addition, the vast majority of fish sold by retailers are young and quite small. This is to your benefit, because these fish are much less expensive than they would be if housed and fed for months until they were significantly larger. When stocking a tank, therefore, you should take the adult sizes of the fish into consideration. An aquarium with a dozen small fish may seem empty at first, but by providing plenty of space for them to grow, the fish will remain healthy and become full-sized adults.

One of your goals is to select fish that prefer different areas in the aquarium in which to swim and feed. A community tank appears more balanced if there are some fish that like to inhabit the upper portion of the aquarium, others that swim in the middle and some that prefer to stay at or near the bottom.

Instead of just glancing at the fish in each tank, take the time to look at them closely. As you observe different kinds of fish, it will become apparent that they differ in habits as well as in physical appearance. For example, as noted earlier, it is best to avoid placing slow-moving fish with species that are fast, nervous swimmers; the quiet, peaceful species become upset by the constant agitation of the faster-moving fish. In addition, some quick swimmers are notorious fin nippers, much to the distress of the slower species.

These differences in personality and behavior can also complicate the maintenance and care of the fish. At feeding time, for example, the fast swimmers will quickly consume most of the food, requiring a second or even a third feeding so that the other fish will have an opportunity to eat. In some cases, the boisterous activity of the active fish will cause the quieter fish to stop eating entirely.

Also avoid keeping together fish that have very different food requirements. Keeping species that are primarily vegetarians with those that need mostly protein increases the difficulty of providing a proper diet that meets the needs of each kind of fish.

A few simple rules to keep fish healthy: Don't overfeed them or overcrowd the tank; change some of the water on a regular basis.

The same principle applies to water chemistry and temperature. Although many species are adaptable to a range of chemical and temperature parameters, keeping fish together that have preferences at either end of the ranges can present difficulties. You are always better off choosing fish that do best under similar aquarium conditions. Many beginning aquarists tend to think of compatibility in community tank fish as involving only personality and behavior, whereas, in reality, compatibility includes all aquarium conditions.

Personality and behavior are important, however. Territoriality and aggressiveness vary among species and even among individuals of the same species. The results of these differences can cause major problems for a fishkeeper. Aggressive fish will chase and harass other fish and will often attempt to control access to food at feeding time. Territorial fish will simply take over one or more sections of a tank and refuse to allow other fish to enter those areas. Although a number of techniques may minimize these kinds of conflicts, it is always better to choose species that are well suited to the typical community aquarium environment.

One rule of fishkeeping that many hobbyists learn the hard way is that most fish will eat whatever fits in

Fish disease is almost always the result of physical stress.

their mouths, including tankmates. Even if young fish are relatively similar in size, this may change as they grow to adulthood. The greater the differences in size, the more likely it is that predation will occur. Fish with large mouths for their size are almost always predatory and can be kept safely only with species of the same size or larger.

It is difficult to list specific combinations of species that will please every hobbyist. In general, however, combinations of tetras, livebearers, and small catfish are usually quite successful and make an attractive display. Because these fish are quite young when purchased, they are difficult to sex, with the exception of the livebearers, in which females and males are easily identified. If the eventual goal is to breed the fish, but the species is difficult to sex, a minimum of six individuals should be purchased to ensure ending up with at least one pair.

BRINGING FISH HOME

Having chosen a modest number of fish for the aquarium, you will arrive home with several plastic bags containing water and fish. Do not combine your trip to the store to buy fish with any other errands unless the fish are purchased last. The small amounts of water in each bag are subject to rapid temperature fluctuation and pollution.

The usual recommendation is to float the bags in the aquarium water for 15 to 30 minutes to equalize the temperatures of the bag water with the tank water before putting the fish into the tank. In reality, however, unless the water in the tank is colder than that in the bags, there is no reason to float them in the tank. You want to get the fish into the tank as quickly as you can. Although the water in the dealer's tanks is probably safe enough, it is better to avoid adding it to your tank water. Therefore, the best procedure for introducing the fish to the tank is to take a large net and place it over a bucket, dump the water and fish into the net and move the netted fish immediately to the aquarium. Discard the water in the bucket.

Leave the tank lights off during the first day the fish are in residence. Do not feed them. This gives the fish time to adjust to their new home. They may hide a lot, but after a day or two they will begin to get used to the tank and will settle down. The caves, nooks, and crannies you created with rocks and the shelter provided by plants will speed this process up. The existence of readily available shelter actually makes the fish hide less because they feel more secure. Eventually, they will spend more and more time out in the open.

If you are adding fish to an existing tank, the new fish should be quarantined for at least two weeks. A small tank, perhaps 10 gallons (38 l) in size, can be placed in an out-of-the-way location. Filtration can consist of a sponge filter, which will provide biological filtration. If the sponge filter is placed in the display tank for a few weeks prior to setting up the quarantine tank, it will be fully populated with nitrifying bacteria by the time it goes into the quarantine tank, thus offering immediate biological filtration. Just add a small heater and a hood with a light and the tank is ready to house the new fish.

By quarantining these fish for at least two weeks, you can be more certain you are not adding diseased fish to your display tank. Remember, physical stress makes fish much more susceptible to disease-causing organisms already in the water. Being netted, bagged, and transported creates enormous amounts of stress on fish, and the only reliable way to minimize the likelihood of triggering disease among the existing aquarium residents of a tank is by isolating the new fish for long enough to determine that they are healthy. During the quarantine period, the new fish should be observed closely for signs of disease.

AQUARIUM MAINTENANCE

Aquarium maintenance, like housework, is necessary. Unlike housework, however, aquarium maintenance is relatively easy and takes little time. In fact, too much maintenance is just as bad as too little. Some aquarists, at the first signs of algae, for example, will completely tear down a tank, vigorously clean everything and then set the tank up again. All of the beneficial nitrifying bacteria are removed when this happens, and the tank must be broken in again, causing great stress to the fish.

Too little maintenance, on the other hand, leads to problems that are no better. The filter clogs, the water becomes laden with dissolved organic waste products, and the tank becomes increasingly dirty.

Assuming that the aquarium is not overstocked with fish and the fish are not overfed, maintenance can be divided into tasks that should be done every week and tasks that are required only once every four to eight weeks. Weekly maintenance consists primarily of siphoning out 10 to 15 percent of the tank water and replacing it with fresh tap water of the same temperature that has been treated with a water conditioner to remove any chlorine or chloramine. Experienced aquarists know that partial water changes are the secret of success in fishkeeping. Novice hobbyists are often under the impression that filter systems eliminate the need to change water, but nothing could be farther from the truth. Some organic compounds that accumulate in the water cannot be removed by filtration but can be reduced by changing some of the water every week.

The other weekly maintenance task is to clean the inside of the front glass. Algae can be removed with a plastic pad or other algae-removing accessory available at your local aquarium store. Unless you find the appearance of algae on the back and side glass extremely unattractive, it should be left where it is. Algae makes an aquarium look more natural, it helps remove nitrate from the water, and some fish will nibble on it. While some algae may be acceptable, excessive amounts can be unattractive. The best way to control the growth of algae is to reduce the levels of nitrate in the water. The easiest and most effective method for doing this is, once again, partial water changes on a weekly basis.

Every four to eight weeks, the outside power filter must be cleaned. The more fish there are in the tank, or the larger the fish are, the more often the filter will need maintenance. If you are using ceramic noodles or rings in the filter for biological filtration, these should be rinsed off very lightly. More thorough cleaning would remove the nitrifying bacteria. The mechanical filtering medium is either rinsed out if it is reusable, or disposed of and replaced. The granular activated carbon is also replaced with new carbon. The old carbon cannot be reused.

One of the reasons why many experienced hobbyists prefer filters that hang on the back of a tank is the ease with which this type of filter can be cleaned and serviced. Canister filters must be disconnected and taken apart completely, making the task of filter maintenance time consuming. As a result, hobbyists tend to avoid servicing canister filters as often as they should. Over time, the canister filter becomes clogged, the flow of water is reduced, and the quality of filtration decreases.

The goal of maintenance is to keep the tank nice looking, and, more important, to make the aquarium as healthy as possible for the fish. A regular program of aquarium maintenance is the first line of defense in the fight against disease in fish.

MISCELLANEOUS GUIDELINES

If a tank is not overstocked, it can withstand any number of circumstances that might otherwise prove more serious. Power failures, for example, will have relatively little effect on a healthy tank. If a power outage occurs during hot weather, the lack of aeration and reduced dissolved oxygen can be serious in heavily stocked aquariums, but otherwise will be only an inconvenience. If power is lost during winter and the entire house relies on electricity for heat, the aquarium water will cool slowly to the room temperature, which will not be a problem unless the fish are already under stress from poor water quality and overcrowding.

Many aquarists have more to worry about if they go on vacation and have a neighbor or friend come in to feed the fish. The horror stories of hobbyists coming home to tanks full of dead fish can usually be traced to well-meaning caretakers who kill the fish with kindness by overfeeding them. If an aquarium is well managed and the fish are healthy, it is generally better to just let the tank run without feeding the fish. The fish can easily go one or two weeks without food. In cases where it is necessary to have someone come in and feed the fish, you should leave packets of food, one for each day's feeding.

Many times, aquarium disasters are the result of factors outside the tank itself. If a room is being painted or sprayed for insects, the air pump should be turned off and the tank covered. Fumes and smoke contain toxic chemicals that can kill fish if pumped into the tank water.

If an aquarium must be moved, the fish will have to be removed from the tank and the tank emptied. An aquarium with gravel and water is very heavy to begin with, and even if it is possible to move it, the resulting physical stress on the tank will result in leaks at joints and even broken glass. Some of the tank water should be siphoned into buckets or other appropriate containers to hold the fish. A one-step water conditioner should be added to the containers. If the fish are being moved far, they should be placed in bags with conditioned tank water, and the bags should then be placed in Styrofoam coolers to provide temperature and physical shock insulation.

WORDS OF ADVICE

As you become more involved with the hobby of aquariums and fish, you will discover that many aquarists and dealers have strong opinions about what it takes to keep fish and how it should be done. There is also a lot of anecdotal information out there, totally lacking in scientific fact.

There are no magic answers. Remember, there can be more than one way to go about setting up a tank. As you gain experience, you will find that some things work better for you than others. Ask questions and listen to the answers carefully. There are many tips and techniques that will be useful to you. No matter how long an aquarist has been in the hobby, there are always new things to learn.

Go slow and be patient. It is easy to start out with one 15-gallon (57-l) tank and end up with dozens of tanks ranging up to a hundred gallons (380 l) or more within a year or two. If you take on more than you have time, room, or money for, it will stop being fun. Instead of trying to maintain and breed many species, specialize. Go to some of the annual shows that aquarium societies put on and see what aquarium fish look like when kept by master aquarists.

Above all, keep your perspective. Fishkeeping is a wonderful hobby, but that is all it is. Many hobbyists make the mistake of thinking that it is a quick and easy step from aquarist to aquarium store retailer. What a great way to make a living! Few hobbyists have the business expertise to make a success of it, and most are ill-prepared to deal with the public.

Many fishkeepers had aquariums as youngsters but drifted away from the hobby during their late teens as college, relationships, and jobs became priorities. They rediscover the hobby years later, often when they have children of their own. Whether you are rediscovering aquariums or just starting out for the first time, relax, enjoy, and have fun!

THE
FISHES
2

THE FISHES

Although literally thousands of species of fish can be kept in aquariums, relatively few are truly suitable for the typical community tank. Even the carefully chosen selection of fish described in this section includes species that are not necessarily compatible with each other, despite the fact that compatibility was a major consideration in choosing which fish to include. Selecting fish is an exercise in judgment. Ask a dozen experienced hobbyists for lists of recommended community aquarium fish and you will get twelve different lists. While many species will appear on all the lists, there will also be a divergence of opinion concerning fish that are likely to be compatible in most community tanks.

The goal of the aquarist is to select fish that are likely to coexist peacefully in the same tank. To increase the odds of success in this process, a number of factors should be taken into consideration. For example, the ideal community fish are hardy, easy to care for, and not too large for the tank.

The information given here, when combined with the discussion on choosing fish in the first part of the book, can help you avoid the most common mistakes made by new hobbyists. It is important to remember that space limitations restrict the amount of information that can be presented in a book of this size. For more detailed information, there are numerous "atlases" of aquarium fish available that cover hundreds of species. Although such books are valuable references, the abbreviated descriptions provided here will be more than adequate for the purposes of setting up a community tank.

The descriptions accompanying each fish are broken down into easily comparable categories that provide essential information about each species. Each category is explained below to help you evaluate the descriptions.

COMMON NAMES

The common names given here are generally used by most retailers, largely because the fish included in this section have been available for years and are well known. With lesser-known species or species identified only by scientific names, however, wholesalers, distributors, and retailers may invent common names. Because a picture is worth a thousand words, sometimes photos in books are the only way to agree upon the identity of a fish.

SCIENTIFIC NAMES

Unlike common names, recognized scientific names will reliably identify a species of fish no matter where you are. The only catch to this is that the classification of fish, known as taxonomy, is revised from time to time by ichthyologists as they learn more about specific groups of fish. Usually, revised editions of aquarium books will reflect the most current scientific names. Despite these occasional changes, scientific names can be relied upon far more than common names. Again, you should have few problems with the fish listed here.

ORIGIN

The origins listed here are generalizations and are not meant to be definitive. The geographic distributions of species can vary widely. For example, a species may be found in a river that traverses several countries or it may be restricted to one locale in one country. This information is of little practical value, although knowing the region or country of origin can sometimes help indicate the type of water chemistry a species is best suited for. In addition, some aquarists like to set up community tanks in which all of the fish are likely to be found together in their natural setting.

LENGTH OF FISH

The length given for each species of fish is the typical maximum size in an aquarium setting and is not necessarily the largest size a fish can grow to in its natural environment. The nutritional value of the diet provided and water quality are crucial to the growth of fish. Fish give off substances that can accumulate in the water and reach concentrations high enough to slow or completely stop growth. Filtration will not remove these substances, but frequent partial water changes will minimize them. The lengths given here are standard lengths, which do not include the tail. In species that exhibit sexual dimorphism, it is not unusual for one gender to be larger or smaller than the other.

TEMPERATURE

In the natural environments of many fish, water temperatures can differ from season to season, at varying depths, and between areas of sun and shade. Therefore, you will notice that a temperature range is given for each species. This is not meant to encourage you to allow tank temperatures to fluctuate over that range. You can use it as a guide to help avoid keeping fish that prefer cooler water with those species that do better in warmer water. When referring to tropical fish, the term *tropical* generally means water temperatures of 68°F (20°C), with the preferred temperatures usually higher.

TANK LENGTH

This measurement should not be confused with the discussion in the first section of the book dealing with stocking levels based on the number of inches of fish to tank volume or aquarium surface area. Tank length represents the shortest dimension recommended to provide sufficient space and swimming room for each species. In the case of the smaller, quieter species, it may be possible to use a shorter tank, but only if stocking levels are kept low.

LOCATION IN TANK

A balanced community aquarium contains fish that swim at different levels in the tank. Each species of fish has a general depth preference in terms of top, middle, or bottom. Sometimes the physical appearance of a fish makes this fairly obvious. Fish with upturned mouths, such as hatchet fish, will feed from the surface, whereas fish with mouths that face downward, such as some catfish, will feed from the bottom. The locations given in the descriptions are generalizations. Fish that prefer one level in a tank will often also occupy the next nearest level as well. Some species have no preference and will wander from top to bottom.

FOODS

Foods are listed in order of preference and convenience. Flake foods, which include freeze-dried foods, are the most convenient and are generally nutritious. Two or three different types of dry foods should be rotated in the diet to help provide the widest possible variety of nutrients. All fish benefit from live foods. Brine shrimp are excellent, providing both substantial amounts of protein and vitamins and an opportunity for the fish to hunt and chase their food. When live foods are difficult to obtain, frozen foods can be substituted. Fish that are partial or total vegetarians must receive adequate amounts of vegetable material, including romaine lettuce, spinach, and zucchini, or squash that is sliced and boiled just long enough so that it sinks. Vegetable flake foods can be used, but should not constitute the only source of vegetable material. Pelletized foods specifically formulated for vegetarian fish are also available. Most bottom-feeding fish will consume pellets and tablet foods that sink. Many fish will nibble on algae, which is an excellent reason for allowing it to grow in the aquarium.

SEXUAL DIMORPHISM

Sexual dimorphism refers to the physical differences between males and females that make it possible to tell them apart. In some species, there are no obvious differences in appearance and thus no way to identify

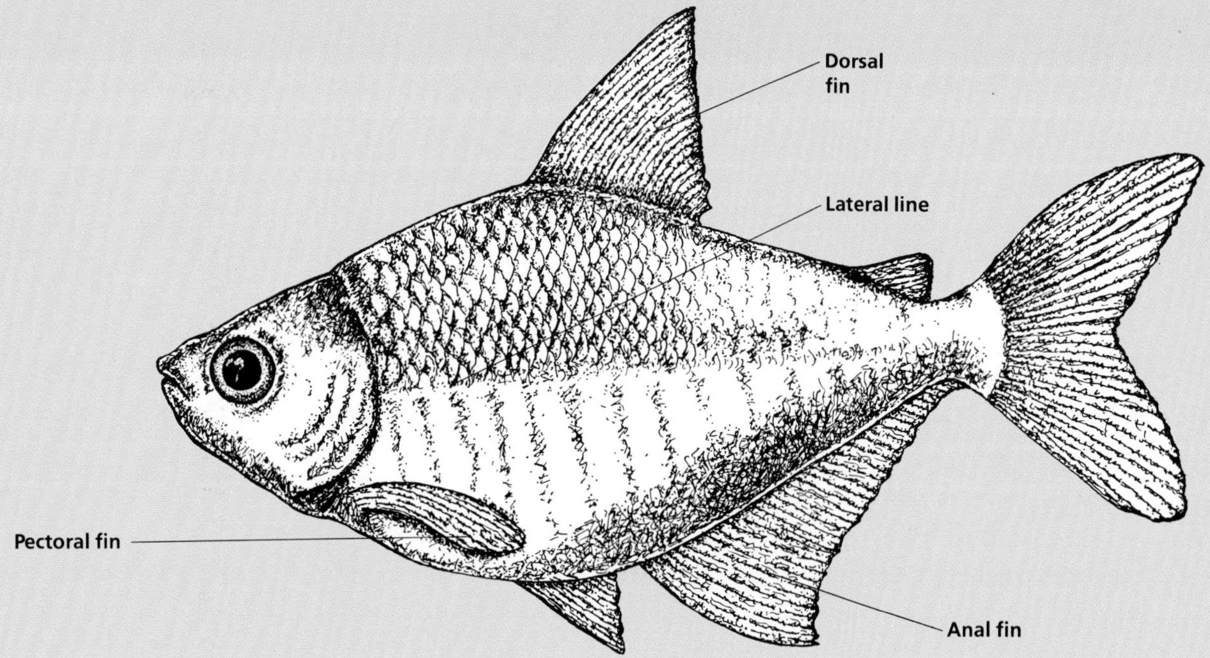
Dorsal fin
Lateral line
Pectoral fin
Anal fin

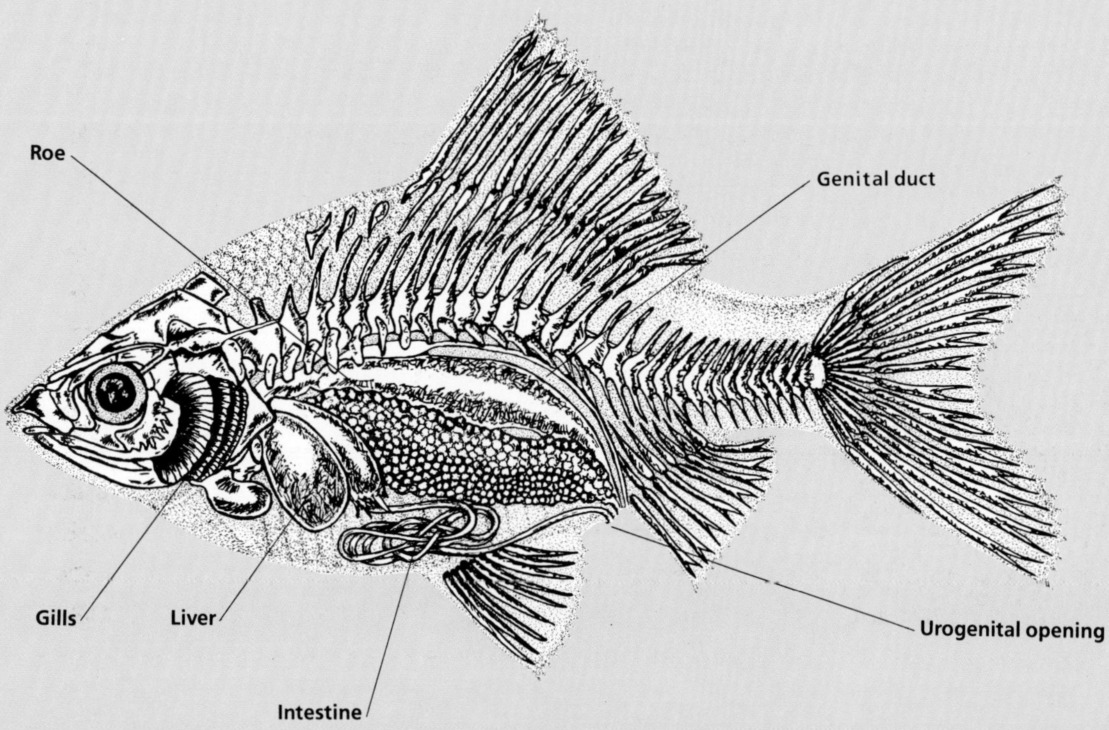
Roe
Genital duct
Gills
Liver
Intestine
Urogenital opening

the sexes. Most species, however, exhibit differences in size, intensity of color, shape of fins, or other distinguishing characteristics that make it possible to tell which is which. Sometimes the differences are obvious, other times they are subtle.

BREEDING

Quite simply, a yes indicates only that the species has been bred in an aquarium, not how easy or difficult the task may be. It is not within the scope of this book to cover this challenging and rewarding aspect of the hobby. Suffice it to say that if you are interested in breeding fish, you should read everything you can about the species you would like to spawn. Some species will do what comes naturally with little help from the aquarist, whereas others require exacting water and tank conditions.

COMMENTS

The comments for each species are intended to provide bits and pieces of information that will be of some value in trying to assemble a compatible combination of fish. Of particular importance are remarks concerning species of fish that tend to school or group together. Many community aquarium fish prefer to school or form groups. These fish have evolved behavioral habits and social interactions that depend on being with members of their own species. Schooling provides a greater sense of security, and many species exhibit normal behavior only when kept in groups. Therefore, these fish should be maintained in groups of at least three to five or more. As a rule, small fish such as tetras, barbs, and rasboras are schooling fish, although this isn't always specifically stated in the comments for each species in a large family of fish.

To help you sort out the most compatible combinations of fish, the comments make note of whether the fish are primarily peaceful, active, or territorial. Peaceful fish should not be kept with active species. The quieter fish will be intimidated by the activity of the fast-swimming fish, and often hide and even refuse to eat. Fish that can be territorial, particularly some species of cichlids, are often relatively peaceful community tank inhabitants until it comes to breeding, at which time they will set up a territory in the tank and keep all other fish outside its boundaries.

The fish listed here are all quite hardy, particularly in comparison with species that are more demanding in terms of water quality or food requirements. However, some of these species are more sensitive to changes in water quality than others, and this fact is noted in the comments. Remember that while all fish should have very good quality water to live in, some species are more tolerant than others if the water quality decreases for one reason or another.

Although these comments are not lengthy, they can help you narrow down your list of fish to those species that seem most likely to be compatible with each other and with the tank you plan to put them in. When in doubt, do not hesitate to consult your local aquarium store or an experienced hobbyist.

THE FISHES

100 EASY-TO-KEEP SPECIES

Common name:	**Siamese Fighting Fish**
Scientific name:	*Betta splendens*
Family:	Belontiidae
Origin:	Thailand and Cambodia
Length of fish:	3 in (8 cm)
Temperature:	76°–86° F (24°–30° C)
Tank length:	10 in (25 cm)
Location in tank:	Top
Foods:	Flake, small pellet, and live foods.
Sexual dimorphism:	Male has larger fins and is more colorful.
Breeding:	Yes
Comments:	Often kept in 1-gallon (3.8-l) bowls. Water quality must be properly maintained and temperature should be kept above 76° F (24° C). Not recommended for community tank because fins are easy target for other fish.

Common name: **Thick-lipped Gourami**

Scientific name: *Colisa labiosa*

Family:	Belontiidae
Origin:	India
Length of fish:	4 in (9 cm)
Temperature:	72°–82° F (22°–28° C)
Tank length:	24 in (61 cm)
Location in tank:	Middle-Top
Foods:	Flake and live foods.
Sexual dimorphism:	Male is more colorful, dorsal fin is longer.
Breeding:	Yes
Comments:	Peaceful fish that is well suited to community tanks. Tank should have enough plants to provide shelter and security for fish. Keep with other quiet species.

Common name:	**Dwarf Gourami** ◀
Scientific name:	*Colisa lalia*
Family:	Belontiidae
Origin:	India
Length of fish:	2 in (5 cm)
Temperature:	72°–82° F (22°–28° C)
Tank length:	24 in (61 cm)
Location in tank:	Middle-Top
Foods:	Vegetable material, algae, flake, and live foods.
Sexual dimorphism:	Male is significantly more colorful.
Breeding:	Yes
Comments:	Small, quiet fish that needs companions of similar temperament if kept in community aquarium. Good water quality is vital to keeping this species healthy.

Common name:	**Honey Gourami** ▶
Scientific name:	*Colisa sota*
Family:	Belontiidae
Origin:	India
Length of fish:	2 in (5 cm)
Temperature:	72°–82° F (22°–28° C)
Tank length:	16 in (41 cm)
Location in tank:	Middle-Top
Foods:	Flake and live foods, some vegetable material.
Sexual dimorphism:	Male is more colorful during spawning.
Breeding:	Yes
Comments:	Peaceful, somewhat timid fish that will only do well in community tank if other fish are of similar temperament. Good water quality is essential.

Common name:	**Paradise Fish**
Scientific name:	*Macropodus opercularis*
Family:	Belontiidae
Origin:	Eastern Asia
Length of fish:	4 in (10 cm)
Temperature:	65°–80° F (18°–26° C)
Tank length:	30 in (76 cm)
Location in tank:	Middle-Bottom
Foods:	Flake, pellet, and live foods.
Sexual dimorphism:	Male has longer fins, is more colorful.
Breeding:	Yes
Comments:	Active fish that needs a large tank. Adult males cannot be kept together. This species was the first tropical fish to be kept in aquariums.

Common name:	**Moonlight Gourami**
Scientific name:	*Trichogaster microlepis*
Family:	Belontiidae
Origin:	Thailand and Cambodia
Length of fish:	6 in (15 cm)
Temperature:	80°–86° F (26°–30° C)
Tank length:	30 in (76 cm)
Location in tank:	Middle-Top
Foods:	Flake and live foods, vegetable material.
Sexual dimorphism:	Male has orange in pelvic fins, female has yellow.
Breeding:	Yes
Comments:	Quiet, peaceful species that needs a fairly large tank with sufficient hiding places. Do not keep with aggressive, fast-swimming fish.

Common name:	**Snake-skinned Gourami**
Scientific name:	*Trichogaster pectoralis*
Family:	Belontiidae
Origin:	Southeast Asia
Length of fish:	8 in (20 cm)
Temperature:	74°–82° F (23°–28° C)
Tank length:	24 in (61 cm)
Location in tank:	Middle-Bottom
Foods:	Flake and live foods.
Sexual dimorphism:	Male has pointed dorsal fin.
Breeding:	Yes
Comments:	Peaceful, quiet fish that is hardy and does well in water chemistry covering a range of hardnesses and pH.

Common name:	**Three-spot Gourami**
Scientific name:	*Trichogaster trichopterus*
Family:	Belontiidae
Origin:	Southeast Asia
Length of fish:	4 in (10 cm)
Temperature:	72°–82° F (22°–28° C)
Tank length:	24 in (61 cm)
Location in tank:	Middle-Top
Foods:	Flake and live foods, vegetable material.
Sexual dimorphism:	Male has pointed dorsal fin.
Breeding:	Yes
Comments:	Extremely quiet species, although only one male should be kept in a tank. Very hardy and easy to maintain.

Common name: **Pearl Gourami**

Scientific name: *Trichogasteri leeri*

Family: Belontiidae

Origin: Far East

Length of fish: 4 in (12 cm)

Temperature: 74°–82° F (24°–28° C)

Tank length: 24 in (61 cm)

Location in tank: Middle-Top

Foods: Flake and live foods, vegetable materials.

Sexual dimorphism: Male has redder, pointed dorsal fin.

Breeding: Yes

Comments: A very hardy, peaceful fish that does well in community aquariums as long as no aggressive species are present.

Common name:	**Croaking Gourami**
Scientific name:	*Trichopsis vittatus*
Family:	Macropodinae
Origin:	India and Southeast Asia
Length of fish:	2.5 in (6 cm)
Temperature:	72°–82° F (22°–28° C)
Tank length:	24 in (61 cm)
Location in tank:	Middle
Foods:	Flake and small live foods.
Sexual dimorphism:	Male is more colorful.
Breeding:	Yes
Comments:	Does well in community tanks with other peaceful fish. Both sexes can make croaking noises.

Common name:	**Kissing Gourami**
Scientific name:	*Helostoma temminckii*
Family:	Helostomatidae
Origin:	Thailand
Length of fish:	12 in (30 cm)
Temperature:	72°–82° F (22°–28° C)
Tank length:	36 in (91 cm)
Location in tank:	Middle-Top
Foods:	Flake and live foods, vegetable material.
Sexual dimorphism:	Difficult to distinguish.
Breeding:	Yes
Comments:	A quiet species that does well in community aquariums. It can grow quite large given good water conditions and frequent water changes.

Common name:	**Indian Glass Fish**
Scientific name:	*Chanda ranga*
Family:	Centropomidae
Origin:	India and Thailand
Length of fish:	3 in (8 cm)
Temperature:	66°–78° F (19°–25° C)
Tank length:	24 in (61 cm)
Location in tank:	Middle
Foods:	Flake foods, but should also receive live or frozen foods.
Sexual dimorphism:	Male has blue edges on fins.
Breeding:	Yes
Comments:	A quiet, almost timid schooling fish that should be kept in a community tank containing other peaceful inhabitants.

Common name:	**Bloodfin**
Scientific name:	*Aphyocharax anisitsi*
Family:	Characidae
Origin:	Argentina
Length of fish:	3 in (8 cm)
Temperature:	70°–82° F (21°–28° C)
Tank length:	24 in (61 cm)
Location in tank:	Middle-Top
Foods:	Flake and live foods, vegetable material.
Sexual dimorphism:	Male has small hook on anal fin.
Breeding:	Yes
Comments:	A very hardy species that should be kept in a school. Although it can live in cool water, its color is best at higher temperatures.

Common name:	**Blind Cavefish** ◀
Scientific name:	*Astyanax fasciatus mexicanus*
Family:	Characidae
Origin:	Mexico and Central America
Length of fish:	3.5 in (9 cm)
Temperature:	68°–78° F (20°–25° C)
Tank length:	30 in (76 cm)
Location in tank:	Middle
Foods:	Flake and live foods.
Sexual dimorphism:	Male is slimmer.
Breeding:	Yes
Comments:	A peaceful community tank species that should be maintained in schools. No special care requirements. Evolved in caves where it lost need for eyes and uses scent to locate food.

Common name:	**Cardinal Tetra** ▶
Scientific name:	*Paracheirodon axelrodi*
Family:	Characidae
Origin:	Brazil and Venezuela
Length of fish:	2 in (5 cm)
Temperature:	74°–82° F (23°–28° C)
Tank length:	24 in (61 cm)
Location in tank:	Middle-Bottom
Foods:	Flake and small live foods.
Sexual dimorphism:	Male is slightly slimmer.
Breeding:	Yes
Comments:	A very popular aquarium fish that is ideal for a community aquarium. A large school presents a striking display.

Common name:	**Black Tetra**
Scientific name:	*Gymnocorymbus ternetzi*
Family:	Characidae
Origin:	Paraguay and Bolivia
Length of fish:	2.2 in (5.5 cm)
Temperature:	70°–80° F (21°–26° C)
Tank length:	24 in (61 cm)
Location in tank:	Middle
Foods:	Flake (including vegetable) and live foods.
Sexual dimorphism:	Anal fin of male is significantly broader.
Breeding:	Yes
Comments:	An excellent fish for a community tank. Does best in schools. Color fades from black to gray by adulthood.

Common name:	**Silver-tipped Tetra**
Scientific name:	*Hasemania nana*
Family:	Characidae
Origin:	Brazil
Length of fish:	2 in (5 cm)
Temperature:	72°–82° F (22°–28° C)
Tank length:	24 in (61 cm)
Location in tank:	Middle
Foods:	Flake and live foods.
Sexual dimorphism:	Male is slimmer, with brighter colors.
Breeding:	Yes
Comments:	A peaceful, schooling fish that is an excellent choice for community tanks. Hardy when water quality is good, but sensitive to deteriorating water quality.

Common name:	**Glowlight Tetra**
Scientific name:	*Hemigrammus erythrozonus*
Family:	Characidae
Origin:	Guyana
Length of fish:	1.5 in (4 cm)
Temperature:	74°–82° F (23°–27° C)
Tank length:	24 in (61 cm)
Location in tank:	Middle
Foods:	Flake and small live foods.
Sexual dimorphism:	Female is larger than male.
Breeding:	Yes
Comments:	As with the majority of tetras, these are excellent aquarium fish, well suited to a community tank.

Common name:	**Head-and-taillight Tetra** ◀
Scientific name:	*Hemigrammus ocellifer*
Family:	Characidae
Origin:	Guyana and Bolivia
Length of fish:	2 in (5 cm)
Temperature:	74°–82° F (23°–28° C)
Tank length:	24 in (61 cm)
Location in tank:	Middle
Foods:	Flake and small live foods.
Sexual dimorphism:	Male's swim bladder is more pointed in appearance.
Breeding:	Yes
Comments:	A peaceful, community tank fish that should be kept in groups. Dark substrate and background emphasize colors of fish.

Common name:	**Rummy-nosed Tetra** ▶
Scientific name:	*Hemigrammus rhodostomus*
Family:	Characidae
Origin:	Brazil
Length of fish:	2 in (5 cm)
Temperature:	74°–80° F (23°–26° C)
Tank length:	24 in (5 cm)
Location in tank:	Middle
Foods:	Flake and small live foods.
Sexual dimorphism:	Male is slimmer.
Breeding:	Yes
Comments:	In a community tank setting, a school of these fish is very attractive. They require very good water quality.

Common name:	**Bleeding-heart Tetra**
Scientific name:	*Hyphessobrycon erythrostigma*
Family:	Characidae
Origin:	Peru
Length of fish:	2.5 in (6 cm)
Temperature:	74°–82° F (23°–28° C)
Tank length:	24 in (61 cm)
Location in tank:	Middle
Foods:	Flake and small live foods.
Sexual dimorphism:	Male has longer dorsal and anal fins.
Breeding:	No
Comments:	A popular tetra that should be kept in groups in a community aquarium with other peaceful species.

Common name:	**Flame Tetra**
Scientific name:	*Hyphessobrycon flammeus*
Family:	Characidae
Origin:	Brazil
Length of fish:	1.5 in (4 cm)
Temperature:	72°–82° F (22°–28° C)
Tank length:	24 in (61 cm)
Location in tank:	Middle
Foods:	Flake and small live foods.
Sexual dimorphism:	Anal fin of male is red.
Breeding:	Yes
Comments:	Another excellent choice for a community setup containing quiet species. When kept under these conditions, the fish exhibit beautiful coloration.

Common name:	**Black Neon Tetra**
Scientific name:	*Hyphessobrycon herbertaxelrodi*
Family:	Characidae
Origin:	Brazil
Length of fish:	1.5 in (4 cm)
Temperature:	72°–82° F (22°–28° C)
Tank length:	24 in (61 cm)
Location in tank:	Middle-Top
Foods:	Flake and small live foods.
Sexual dimorphism:	Stomach of female is rounder.
Breeding:	Yes
Comments:	Requires a balanced diet and very good water quality to do well. Should be kept in schools in a community tank.

Common name:	**Lemon Tetra**
Scientific name:	*Hyphessobrycon pulchripinnis*
Family:	Characidae
Origin:	Brazil
Length of fish:	2 in (5 cm)
Temperature:	72°–82° F (22°–28° C)
Tank length:	24 in (61 cm)
Location in tank:	Middle-Top
Foods:	Flake and small live foods.
Sexual dimorphism:	Anal fin of male has broad, black edge.
Breeding:	Yes
Comments:	When kept in a school in a community tank that has dark substrate and background, the color of this fish is quite beautiful.

Common name: **Black Phantom Tetra**
Scientific name: *Megalamphodus megalopterus*

Family:	Characidae
Origin:	Brazil
Length of fish:	2 in (5 cm)
Temperature:	72°–82° F (22°–28° C)
Tank length:	24 in (61 cm)
Location in tank:	Middle
Foods:	Flake and small live foods.
Sexual dimorphism:	Male has black fins, female has red.
Breeding:	Yes
Comments:	A very hardy species that is an excellent addition to a community tank. Can be kept in pairs or groups.

Common name: **Red Phantom Tetra**

Scientific name: *Megalamphodus sweglesi*

Family:	Characidae
Origin:	Colombia
Length of fish:	1.5 in (4 cm)
Temperature:	68°–74° F (20°–23° C)
Tank length:	24 in (61 cm)
Location in tank:	Middle
Foods:	Flake and small live foods.
Sexual dimorphism:	Red, black, and white in male's dorsal fin.
Breeding:	Yes
Comments:	A very peaceful species that should be kept with fish of similar disposition that also prefer slightly cooler water.

Common name:	**Diamond Tetra**
Scientific name:	*Moenkhausia pitteri*
Family:	Characidae
Origin:	Venezuela
Length of fish:	2.5 in (6 cm)
Temperature:	76°–82° F (24°–28° C)
Tank length:	24 in (61 cm)
Location in tank:	Middle
Foods:	Flake and small live foods.
Sexual dimorphism:	Male has larger, pointed dorsal fin.
Breeding:	Yes
Comments:	A good fish for community tanks as long as the water is not too hard. Needs open areas for swimming. Color most intense against dark background.

Common name:	**Red-eye Tetra**
Scientific name:	*Moenkhausia sanctaefilomenae*
Family:	Characidae
Origin:	Peru, Brazil, and Bolivia
Length of fish:	2.75 in (7 cm)
Temperature:	72°–80° F (22°–26° C)
Tank length:	30 in (76 cm)
Location in tank:	Middle
Foods:	Flake and small live foods.
Sexual dimorphism:	Stomach of female more rounded than male's.
Breeding:	Yes
Comments:	Active but peaceful community tank fish that is hardy and easy to keep. Like many tetras, can live in hard water but only breeds in soft water.

Common name:	**Emperor Tetra**
Scientific name:	*Nematobrycon palmeri*
Family:	Characidae
Origin:	Colombia
Length of fish:	2 in (5 cm)
Temperature:	72°–82° F (22°–28° C)
Tank length:	24 in (61 cm)
Location in tank:	Middle
Foods:	Flake and small live foods.
Sexual dimorphism:	Fins of male are longer, more pointed.
Breeding:	Yes
Comments:	A very hardy species, but only if excellent water quality is maintained. Should only be kept with other peaceful species.

Common name:	**Neon Tetra**
Scientific name:	*Paracheirodon innesi*
Family:	Characidae
Origin:	Peru
Length of fish:	1.5 in (4 cm)
Temperature:	68°–80° F (20°–26° C)
Tank length:	24 in (61 cm)
Location in tank:	Middle-Bottom
Foods:	Flake and small live foods.
Sexual dimorphism:	Male is slimmer.
Breeding:	Yes
Comments:	Perhaps the most popular of all aquarium fish. Very peaceful and well suited for community tanks as long as the other fish are not too large.

Common name: **Congo Tetra**

Scientific name: *Phenacogrammus interruptus*

Family:	Characidae
Origin:	Zaire
Length of fish:	3 in (8 cm)
Temperature:	75°–82° F (22°–28° C)
Tank length:	30 in (76 cm)
Location in tank:	Middle-Top
Foods:	Flake and live foods.
Sexual dimorphism:	Male is larger, fins longer.
Breeding:	Yes
Comments:	A beautiful tetra from Africa. A timid fish that should be kept only with other quiet species. Should be housed in a medium-sized tank of 20 gallons (76 l) or more.

Common name:	**X-ray Fish**
Scientific name:	*Pristella maxillaris*
Family:	Characidae
Origin:	Venezuela and Brazil
Length of fish:	2 in (5 cm)
Temperature:	74°–82° F (24°–28° C)
Tank length:	24 in (61 cm)
Location in tank:	Middle
Foods:	Flake (including vegetable) and live foods.
Sexual dimorphism:	Male is more slender than female.
Breeding:	Yes
Comments:	A peaceful community fish that looks best when kept in water that is soft to moderately hard, with moderate amounts of light.

Common name:	**Penguin Fish**
Scientific name:	*Thayeria obliqua*
Family:	Characidae
Origin:	Brazil
Length of fish:	3 in (8 cm)
Temperature:	72°–82° F (22°–28° C)
Tank length:	30 in (76 cm)
Location in tank:	Middle-Top
Foods:	Flake and live foods.
Sexual dimorphism:	Stomach of female more rounded prior to spawning.
Breeding:	Yes
Comments:	An excellent choice for a community tank of peaceful inhabitants. Requires very good water quality.

Common name:	**Bronze Corydoras**
Scientific name:	*Corydoras aeneus*
Family:	Callichthyidae
Origin:	Venezuela
Length of fish:	3 in (7 cm)
Temperature:	72°–80° F (22°–26° C)
Tank length:	24 in (61 cm)
Location in tank:	Bottom
Foods:	Flake, pelletized, tablet, and live foods.
Sexual dimorphism:	Male is slimmer, female has deeper body.
Breeding:	Yes
Comments:	All *Corydoras* species are popular among hobbyists. Excellent community residents. Hardy, but must receive same balanced, nutritious diet that is provided to other types of fish.

Common name:	**Skunk Corydoras**
Scientific name:	*Corydoras arcuatus*
Family:	Callichthyidae
Origin:	Brazil and Peru
Length of fish:	2 in (5 cm)
Temperature:	72°–80° F (22°–26° C)
Tank length:	24 in (61 cm)
Location in tank:	Bottom
Foods:	Flake, pelletized, tablet, and live foods.
Sexual dimorphism:	Male is slimmer, female is deeper-bodied.
Breeding:	Yes
Comments:	All *Corydoras* species are suitable for community tanks. Avoid gravel with sharp edges, which will cut barbels, leading to infection.

Common name:	**Leopard Corydoras**
Scientific name:	*Corydoras julii*
Family:	Callichthyidae
Origin:	Brazil
Length of fish:	2 in (5 cm)
Temperature:	72°–80° F (22°–26° C)
Tank length:	24 in (61 cm)
Location in tank:	Bottom
Foods:	Flake, pelletized, tablet, and live foods.
Sexual dimorphism:	Female is deeper-bodied than male.
Breeding:	Yes
Comments:	*Corydoras* are social and do best when kept in groups. Live foods that fall to bottom of tank are eagerly consumed.

Common name:	**Black-spotted Corydoras**
Scientific name:	*Corydoras melanistius*
Family:	Callichthyidae
Origin:	Guyana
Length of fish:	2 in (5 cm)
Temperature:	72°–78° F (22°–25° C)
Tank length:	24 in (61 cm)
Location in tank:	Bottom
Foods:	Flake, pelletized, tablet, and live foods.
Sexual dimorphism:	Male is slimmer than female.
Breeding:	Yes
Comments:	*Corydoras* will breed if housed in a roomy tank in a group and fed a highly nutritious, balanced diet.

Common name: **Reticulated Corydoras**

Scientific name: *Corydoras reticulatus*

Family:	Callichthyidae
Origin:	Peru
Length of fish:	2 in (5 cm)
Temperature:	72°–80° F (22°–26° C)
Tank length:	24 in (61 cm)
Location in tank:	Bottom
Foods:	Flake, pelletized, tablet, and live foods.
Sexual dimorphism:	Female is larger than male.
Breeding:	Yes
Comments:	*Corydoras* have armor plates rather than scales, making them somewhat more resistant to disease, although they do require good water quality.

Common name:	**Flag-tailed Catfish** ◀
Scientific name:	*Dianema urostriata*
Family:	Callichthyidae
Origin:	Brazil
Length of fish:	5 in (13 cm)
Temperature:	72°–80° F (22°–26° C)
Tank length:	36 in (91 cm)
Location in tank:	Bottom
Foods:	Tablet and live foods.
Sexual dimorphism:	Unknown
Breeding:	Yes
Comments:	A peaceful community fish that does best when kept with other members of its species. Mostly active at night.

Common name:	**Plecostomus** ▶
Scientific name:	*Hypostomus plecostomus*
Family:	Loricariidae
Origin:	Brazil
Length of fish:	12 in (30 cm)
Temperature:	72°–82° F (22°–28° C)
Tank length:	48 in (122 cm)
Location in tank:	Bottom
Foods:	Vegetable material, algae, flake, tablet, and pellet foods.
Sexual dimorphism:	Unknown
Breeding:	No
Comments:	Although most often available when very small, this sucker-mouth catfish will grow quite large with proper diet and good water quality. Peaceful, mostly active at night.

Common name: **Dwarf Otocinclus**

Scientific name: *Otocinclus affinis*

Family:	Loricariidae
Origin:	Brazil
Length of fish:	1.5 in (4 cm)
Temperature:	68°–80° F (20°–26° C)
Tank length:	24 in (61 cm)
Location in tank:	Bottom
Foods:	Vegetable material, tablet foods.
Sexual dimorphism:	Female is larger.
Breeding:	Yes
Comments:	A small, peaceful catfish that is compatible with all community fish that are quiet and unaggressive.

Common name:	**Clown Plecostomus**
Scientific name:	*Peckoltia* sp.
Family:	Loricariidae
Origin:	Brazil
Length of fish:	5 in (12.5 cm)
Temperature:	72°–80°F (22°–26°C)
Tank length:	24 in (61 cm)
Location in tank:	Bottom
Foods:	Vegetable material and algae; flake, tablet, and pellet foods.
Sexual dimorphism:	Unknown
Breeding:	Unknown
Comments:	Must have significant amounts of algae to remain healthy. Peaceful species that should have daytime hiding places.

Common name:	**Royal Plecostomus**
Scientific name:	*Panaque nigrolineatus*
Family:	Loricariidae
Origin:	Colombia
Length of fish:	10 in (25 cm)
Temperature:	72°–80°F (22°–26°C)
Tank length:	36 in (91 cm)
Location in tank:	Bottom
Foods:	Vegetable material and algae; flake, tablet, and pellet foods.
Sexual dimorphism:	Unknown
Breeding:	Unknown
Comments:	A striking, peaceful fish that requires excellent water quality and a lot of vegetable matter in its diet. Can grow somewhat large but is not particularly active.

Common name:	**Whiptail Loricaria**
Scientific name:	*Rineloricaria fallax*
Family:	Loricariidae
Origin:	Paraguay
Length of fish:	4.5 in (11 cm)
Temperature:	60°–78° F (15°–25° C)
Tank length:	30 in (76 cm)
Location in tank:	Bottom
Foods:	Algae, vegetable material, flake, pellet, and tablet foods.
Sexual dimorphism:	Unknown
Breeding:	Yes
Comments:	Suitable for community tanks if water quality is very good and an adequate vegetable diet is provided.

Common name:	**Talking Catfish** ◀
Scientific name:	*Acanthodoras spinosissimus*
Family:	Doradidae
Origin:	Ecuador and Peru
Length of fish:	6 in (15 cm)
Temperature:	68°–80° F (20°–26° C)
Tank length:	36 in (91 cm)
Location in tank:	Bottom
Foods:	Tablet and live foods.
Sexual dimorphism:	Unknown
Breeding:	No
Comments:	Hides during day unless light is subdued. A peaceful species that is compatible with most community fish unless they are very small.

Common name:	**African Glass Catfish** ▶
Scientific name:	*Eutropiellus debauwi*
Family:	Schilbeidae
Origin:	Zaire
Length of fish:	3 in (8 cm)
Temperature:	76°–82° F (24°–28° C)
Tank length:	30 in (76 cm)
Location in tank:	Middle-Top
Foods:	Flake and small live foods.
Sexual dimorphism:	Female is deeper-bodied.
Breeding:	Unknown
Comments:	A peaceful, schooling fish that is active during the day, unlike many catfish. Should be kept in groups. Suitable for most community aquariums.

Common name:	**Glass Catfish**
Scientific name:	*Kryptopterus bicirrhus*
Family:	Silurdae
Origin:	India and Southeast Asia
Length of fish:	6 in (15 cm)
Temperature:	70°–80° F (21°–26° C)
Tank length:	30 in (76 cm)
Location in tank:	Middle
Foods:	Flake and small live foods.
Sexual dimorphism:	Unknown
Breeding:	Yes
Comments:	A peaceful fish that does best when in groups. Can be kept with other quiet species. Needs strong filtration and excellent water quality.

Common name:	**Upside-down Catfish**
Scientific name:	*Synodontis nigriventris*
Family:	Mochokidae
Origin:	Zaire
Length of fish:	4 in (10 cm)
Temperature:	72°–80° F (22°–26° C)
Tank length:	24 in (61 cm)
Location in tank:	All areas
Foods:	Pellet, tablet, and live foods.
Sexual dimorphism:	Female is lighter in color, rounder.
Breeding:	Yes
Comments:	Very peaceful species that should have suitable hiding places. Often hides during the day.

Common name:	**Flag Cichlid**
Scientific name:	*Aequidens curviceps*

Family:	Cichlidae
Origin:	Amazon basin
Length of fish:	3.5 in (9 cm)
Temperature:	72°–80° F (22°–26° C)
Tank length:	24 in (61 cm)
Location in tank:	Middle-Bottom
Foods:	Flake and live foods.
Sexual dimorphism:	Male is larger, with longer dorsal and anal fins.
Breeding:	Yes
Comments:	As with many cichlids, this species may be kept in a community tank until ready for spawning, at which time the pair can be placed in its own tank.

Common name:	**Keyhole Cichlid** ◀
Scientific name:	*Aequidens maronii*
Family:	Cichlidae
Origin:	Guyana
Length of fish:	6 in (15 cm)
Temperature:	72°–78° F (22°–25° C)
Tank length:	30 in (76 cm)
Location in tank:	Middle-Bottom
Foods:	Flake and live foods.
Sexual dimorphism:	Difficult; male's anal fin is usually longer.
Breeding:	Yes
Comments:	One of the most peaceful cichlids and therefore suitable for a community tank. Use plants to provide hiding places for fish.

Common name:	**Port Acara** ▶
Scientific name:	*Aequidens portalegrensis*
Family:	Cichlidae
Origin:	Southern Brazil, Bolivia, and Paraguay
Length of fish:	6 in (15 cm)
Temperature:	62°–74° F (17°–23°C)
Tank length:	36 in (91 cm)
Location in tank:	Middle-Bottom
Foods:	Flake, tablet, and live foods.
Sexual dimorphism:	Yes, but very difficult.
Breeding:	Yes
Comments:	Peaceful but territorial. Breeding pair should have own tank. Do not keep with small fish.

Common name: **Blue Acara**

Scientific name: *Aquidens pulcher*

Family:	Cichlidae
Origin:	Venezuela and Colombia
Length of fish:	8 in (20 cm)
Temperature:	64°–74° F (18°–23°C)
Tank length:	36 in (91 cm)
Location in tank:	Middle-Bottom
Foods:	Flake, tablet, and live foods.
Sexual dimorphism:	Yes, but difficult.
Breeding:	Yes
Comments:	Peaceful but territorial. Power filter and frequent partial water changes necessary. Do not keep with small fish.

Common name:	**Agassiz' Dwarf Cichlid**
Scientific name:	*Apistogramma agassizii*
Family:	Cichlidae
Origin:	Amazon basin
Length of fish:	3 in (8 cm)
Temperature:	72°–76° F (22°–24° C)
Tank length:	24 in (61 cm)
Location in tank:	Middle-Bottom
Foods:	Flake, tablet, and live foods.
Sexual dimorphism:	Males are larger, more colorful, with longer fins.
Breeding:	Yes
Comments:	Peaceful but territorial. Relatively hardy unless water quality deteriorates. Water should be well aerated, with frequent partial water changes.

Common name:	**Borelli's Dwarf Cichlid**
Scientific name:	*Apistogramma borelli*
Family:	Cichlidae
Origin:	Southern Brazil
Length of fish:	3 in (8 cm)
Temperature:	74°–78° F (23°–26°C)
Tank length:	24 in (61 cm)
Location in tank:	Middle-Bottom
Foods:	Freeze-dried and live foods; some flake foods.
Sexual dimorphism:	Males are larger, much more colorful, and have pointed fins.
Breeding:	Yes
Comments:	Peaceful but territorial. Very good water quality essential at all times. It is best to have some fishkeeping experience before attempting to keep dwarf cichlids.

Common name:	**Zebra Cichlid** ◀
Scientific name:	*Pseudotropheus zebra*
Family:	Cichlidae
Origin:	Lake Malawi, East Africa
Length of fish:	6 in (15 cm)
Temperature:	72°–82° F (22°–28° C)
Tank length:	30 in (76 cm)
Location in tank:	Middle-Bottom
Foods:	Flake and live foods, vegetable material and algae.
Sexual dimorphism:	Males have distinctive egg spots on anal fin.
Breeding:	Yes
Comments:	Does well in hard, alkaline water. Very territorial. Provide rockwork for aquascaping. Tank should contain several females for each male.

Common name:	**Jewel Cichlid** ▶
Scientific name:	*Hemichromis bimaculatus*
Family:	Cichlidae
Origin:	Africa
Length of fish:	6 in (15 cm)
Temperature:	70°–74° F (21°–23° C)
Tank length:	30 in (76 cm)
Location in tank:	Bottom
Foods:	Flake, pellet, tablet, and live foods.
Sexual dimorphism:	Difficult to determine.
Breeding:	Yes
Comments:	Peaceful but can be territorial. When kept in a community setting, other fish should be of similar size. Will move gravel during spawning period.

Common name:	**Lifalili Cichlid**
Scientific name:	*Hemichromis lifalili*
Family:	Cichlidae
Origin:	Zaire
Length of fish:	4 in (10 cm)
Temperature:	72°–76° F (22°–23° C)
Tank length:	30 in (76 cm)
Location in tank:	Bottom
Foods:	Flake, pellet, tablet, and live foods.
Sexual dimorphism:	Difficult to determine.
Breeding:	Yes
Comments:	As with many cichlids, this small species can be territorial, particularly during spawning. Not compatible with very small fish.

Common name:	**Severum**
Scientific name:	*Heros severus*
Family:	Cichlidae
Origin:	Amazon basin
Length of fish:	8 in (20 cm)
Temperature:	72°–78° F (22°–25° C)
Tank length:	36 in (91 cm)
Location in tank:	Bottom
Foods:	Flake, live, and frozen foods.
Sexual dimorphism:	Difficult to determine.
Breeding:	Yes
Comments:	Although capable of growing to a comparatively large size, this species is peaceful. Will become territorial during spawning and should be kept only with suitably larger-sized fish.

Common name:	**Festivum**
Scientific name:	*Mesonauta festiva*

Family:	Cichlidae
Origin:	Amazon basin and Guyana
Length of fish:	6 in (15 cm)
Temperature:	72°–78° F (22°–25° C)
Tank length:	36 in (91 cm)
Location in tank:	Middle-Bottom
Foods:	Flake, pellet, and live foods; vegetable material.
Sexual dimorphism:	Difficult to determine.
Breeding:	Yes
Comments:	A peaceful, nervous species that can be kept in a community tank with other peaceful fish that are not small enough to be eaten. Good water quality is important.

Common name: **Dwarf Rainbow Cichlid**
Scientific name: *Pelvicachromis pulcher*

Family:	Cichlidae
Origin:	Nigeria
Length of fish:	4 in (10 cm)
Temperature:	74°–78° F (24°–25° C)
Tank length:	24 in (61 cm)
Location in tank:	Bottom
Foods:	Flake and live foods.
Sexual dimorphism:	Male has pointed anal fin and longer tail fin.
Breeding:	Yes
Comments:	Peaceful dwarf cichlid that is territorial but can be kept with other fish if tank is at least 20 gallons (76 l).

Common name:	**Angelfish** ◄
Scientific name:	*Pterophyllum scalare*
Family:	Cichlidae
Origin:	Amazon basin
Length of fish:	6 in (15 cm)
Temperature:	74°–82° F (23°–28° C)
Tank length:	30 in (76 cm)
Location in tank:	Middle
Foods:	Flake and live foods; vegetable material.
Sexual dimorphism:	None
Breeding:	Yes
Comments:	A perennial favorite that has been selectively bred for numerous colors and patterns. Requires a deep tank (at least 15 inches [37 cm]). Good community aquarium inhabitant if other fish are quiet and peaceful.

Common name:	**Firemouth Cichlid** ►
Scientific name:	*Thorichthys meeki*
Family:	Cichlidae
Origin:	Guatemala
Length of fish:	6 in (15 cm)
Temperature:	70°–76° F (21°–24° C)
Tank length:	30 in (76 cm)
Location in tank:	Bottom
Foods:	Flake, pellet, tablet, and live foods.
Sexual dimorphism:	Male is more colorful, with pointed anal and dorsal fins.
Breeding:	Yes
Comments:	A peaceful cichlid suitable for community tanks except when spawning. Due to aggressive territoriality when breeding, pairs should be moved to their own tank.

Common name:	**Kuhli Loach**
Scientific name:	*Acanthophthalmus kuhli*
Family:	Cobitidae
Origin:	Southeast Asia
Length of fish:	4 in (12 cm)
Temperature:	74°–86° F (23°–30° C)
Tank length:	24 in (61 cm)
Location in tank:	Bottom
Foods:	Tablet and live foods.
Sexual dimorphism:	Unknown
Breeding:	Yes
Comments:	Active primarily at night. Aquarium should have subdued lighting. This species should be fed just before turning off lights.

Common name:	**Clown Loach**
Scientific name:	*Botia macracantha*
Family:	Cobitidae
Origin:	Indonesia and Sumatra
Length of fish:	7 in (18 cm)
Temperature:	76°–86° F (24°–30° C)
Tank length:	36 in (91 cm)
Location in tank:	Bottom
Foods:	Flake, pellet, tablet, frozen, and live foods.
Sexual dimorphism:	Male is larger and tail fin is longer.
Breeding:	No
Comments:	A popular community tank fish that is active but peaceful. This species will control snails in a tank. Can reach a foot in length in natural setting, but seldom more than half that in an aquarium.

Common name:	**Hora's Loach**
Scientific name:	*Botia morleti*

Family:	Cobitidae
Origin:	India and Thailand
Length of fish:	4 in (10 cm)
Temperature:	78°–86° F (24°–30° C)
Tank length:	30 in (76 cm)
Location in tank:	Bottom
Foods:	Tablet, frozen, and live foods.
Sexual dimorphism:	Unknown
Breeding:	No
Comments:	An active but peaceful fish that is suited for community tanks containing other active fish. Hides during the day, comes out at dusk.

Common name: **Dwarf Loach**
Scientific name: *Botia sidthimunki*

Family:	Cobitidae
Origin:	India and Thailand
Length of fish:	2 in (5 cm)
Temperature:	78°–82° F (25°–28° C)
Tank length:	24 in (61 cm)
Location in tank:	Bottom
Foods:	Flake and live foods.
Sexual dimorphism:	None
Breeding:	No
Comments:	A peaceful, schooling species that is highly recommended for community tanks. Is active during the day.

Common name:	**Bala Shark**
Scientific name:	*Balantiocheilus melanopterus*
Family:	Cyprinidae
Origin:	Southeast Asia
Length of fish:	6 in (15 cm)
Temperature:	72°–82° F (22°–28° C)
Tank length:	36 in (91 cm)
Location in tank:	All
Foods:	Flake and live foods; vegetable material.
Sexual dimorphism:	None
Breeding:	No
Comments:	A peaceful fish that can be kept safely with smaller species. Grows to a foot (30 cm) in length in natural environment, half that in aquarium. Is active and needs long tank for swimming. Jumps, so tank must be covered.

Common name:	**Rosy Barb**
Scientific name:	*Barbus conchonius*
Family:	Cyprinidae
Origin:	India
Length of fish:	6 in (15 cm)
Temperature:	64°–72° F (18°–22° C)
Tank length:	30 in (76 cm)
Location in tank:	All
Foods:	Flake, frozen, and live foods.
Sexual dimorphism:	Male is slimmer.
Breeding:	Yes
Comments:	An excellent community fish, but does best with species that also prefer cooler water temperatures.

Common name:	**Clown Barb**
Scientific name:	*Barbus everetti*
Family:	Cyprinidae
Origin:	Southeast Asia
Length of fish:	4 in (10 cm)
Temperature:	74°–86° F (23°–30° C)
Tank length:	30 in (76 cm)
Location in tank:	Bottom
Foods:	Flake and live foods; vegetable material.
Sexual dimorphism:	Female is larger; male is more brightly colored.
Breeding:	Yes
Comments:	Excellent addition to a community tank containing active fish that prefer warmer water.

Common name:	**Banded Barb**
Scientific name:	*Barbus fasciatus*
Family:	Cyprinidae
Origin:	Southeast Asia
Length of fish:	6 in (15 cm)
Temperature:	72°–80° F (22°–26° C)
Tank length:	36 in (91 cm)
Location in tank:	Middle-Bottom
Foods:	Flake and live foods; vegetable material.
Sexual dimorphism:	Females are smaller, slimmer.
Breeding:	Yes
Comments:	Rather active species that should not be kept with quieter, slow-swimming fish. Tank should have both hiding places and open swimming areas.

Common name:	**Black-spot Barb**
Scientific name:	*Barbus filamentosus*
Family:	Cyprinidae
Origin:	India
Length of fish:	6 in (15 cm)
Temperature:	68°–76° F (20°–24° C)
Tank length:	36 in (91 cm)
Location in tank:	Middle
Foods:	Flake and live foods; vegetable material.
Sexual dimorphism:	Male is smaller, more colorful.
Breeding:	Yes
Comments:	Can be kept with other active, fast-swimming fish. Tank should be long, with open swimming area.

Common name:	**Golden Dwarf Barb**
Scientific name:	*Barbus gelius*
Family:	Cyprinidae
Origin:	India
Length of fish:	1.5 in (4 cm)
Temperature:	64°–72° F (18°–22° C)
Tank length:	24 in (61 cm)
Location in tank:	Middle
Foods:	Flake and live foods; vegetable material.
Sexual dimorphism:	Male is slimmer and smaller.
Breeding:	Yes
Comments:	A peaceful, quiet fish that can be kept with other species of similar temperament.

Common name:	**Ruby-headed Barb**
Scientific name:	*Barbus nigrofasciatus*
Family:	Cyprinidae
Origin:	Sri Lanka
Length of fish:	2.5 in (6 cm)
Temperature:	72°–80° F (22°–26° C)
Tank length:	30 in (76 cm)
Location in tank:	Middle
Foods:	Flake and live foods; vegetable material.
Sexual dimorphism:	Male is larger, with more color.
Breeding:	Yes
Comments:	An active, schooling species that should only be kept with other lively fish. Like many barbs, colors are most prominent during spawning.

Common name:	**Checkered Barb**
Scientific name:	*Barbus oligolepis*
Family:	Cyprinidae
Origin:	Indonesia and Sumatra
Length of fish:	6 in (15 cm)
Temperature:	68°–74° F (20°–24° C)
Tank length:	30 in (76 cm)
Location in tank:	Bottom-Middle
Foods:	Flake foods; vegetable material.
Sexual dimorphism:	Male is larger, more colorful.
Breeding:	Yes
Comments:	A good community fish that should be kept in groups. Needs open area in tank for swimming.

Common name:	**Cherry Barb**
Scientific name:	*Barbus titteya*
Family:	Cyprinidae
Origin:	Sri Lanka
Length of fish:	2 in (5 cm)
Temperature:	72°–80° F (22°–26° C)
Tank length:	24 in (61 cm)
Location in tank:	Bottom-Middle
Foods:	Flake and live foods; vegetable material.
Sexual dimorphism:	Male is larger.
Breeding:	Yes
Comments:	Can be kept in a community setup, but may not do well if tankmates include other members of its own species.

Common name:	**Pearl Danio**
Scientific name:	*Brachydanio albolineatus*
Family:	Cyprinidae
Origin:	Southeast Asia
Length of fish:	2.5 in (6 cm)
Temperature:	68°–78° F (20°–25° C)
Tank length:	30 in (76 cm)
Location in tank:	All
Foods:	Flake and live foods.
Sexual dimorphism:	Male is larger, female more colorful.
Breeding:	Yes
Comments:	A very active species that needs a long tank with a large swimming area. Should not be kept with slow-swimming species.

Common name:	**Zebra Danio**
Scientific name:	*Brachydanio rerio*
Family:	Cyprinidae
Origin:	India
Length of fish:	2.5 in (6 cm)
Temperature:	64°–74° F (18°–24° C)
Tank length:	30 in (76 cm)
Location in tank:	All
Foods:	Flake, live, and frozen foods; vegetable material.
Sexual dimorphism:	Male is larger.
Breeding:	Yes
Comments:	Very active schooling species that should be kept only with other fish that are also fast swimmers.

Common name:	**Giant Danio**
Scientific name:	*Danio aequipinnatus*
Family:	Cyprinidae
Origin:	Western India
Length of fish:	4 in (10 cm)
Temperature:	60°–80° F (16°–27° C)
Tank length:	30 in (76 cm)
Location in tank:	All
Foods:	Flake, freeze-dried, tablet, and flake foods; some vegetable material.
Sexual dimorphism:	Male is thinner than female.
Breeding:	Yes
Comments:	Very active species that needs open area in tank for swimming. Should not be kept with quieter species. Does best when in group of six or more.

Common name:	**Flying Fox**
Scientific name:	*Epalzeorhynchus kallopterus*
Family:	Cyprinidae
Origin:	Asia
Length of fish:	6 in (15 cm)
Temperature:	74°–80° F (23°–26° C)
Tank length:	30 in (76 cm)
Location in tank:	Bottom
Foods:	Flake and live foods; vegetable material.
Sexual dimorphism:	Unknown
Breeding:	No
Comments:	Peaceful but can be territorial. Generally suitable for a community tank if aquarium is large enough, perhaps 30 gallons (114 l).

Common name:	**Red-tailed Shark**
Scientific name:	*Epalzeorhyndus (Labeo) bicolor*
Family:	Cyprinidae
Origin:	Thailand
Length of fish:	5 in (13 cm)
Temperature:	72°–80° F (23°–28° C)
Tank length:	30 in (76 cm)
Location in tank:	Middle-Bottom
Foods:	Flake and live foods, algae and vegetable material.
Sexual dimorphism:	Male is more colorful, dorsal fin pointed.
Breeding:	No
Comments:	Smaller individuals are fine for community tank, but adults can become too aggressive. Only one to a tank.

Albino

Common name:	**Red-tailed Rasbora**
Scientific name:	*Rasbora borapetenis*
Family:	Cyprinidae
Origin:	Southeast Asia
Length of fish:	2 in (5 cm)
Temperature:	72°–80° F (22°–26° C)
Tank length:	24 in (61 cm)
Location in tank:	Middle
Foods:	Flake and live foods.
Sexual dimorphism:	Female is slimmer.
Breeding:	Yes
Comments:	A peaceful, schooling species that can be kept in a community tank with other fish of similar behavior.

Common name:	**Elegant Rasbora**
Scientific name:	*Rasbora elegans*
Family:	Cyprinidae
Origin:	Southeast Asia
Length of fish:	8 in (20 cm)
Temperature:	72°–78° F (22°–25° C)
Tank length:	36 in (91 cm)
Location in tank:	Middle
Foods:	Flake and live foods; vegetable material.
Sexual dimorphism:	Female appears larger during spawning period.
Breeding:	Yes
Comments:	A peaceful fish that grows larger than other species of rasbora. Should be kept in groups.

Common name:	**Espes Rasbora**
Scientific name:	*Rasbora espei*
Family:	Cyprinidae
Origin:	Thailand
Length of fish:	1.75 in (4 cm)
Temperature:	72°–82° F (22°–28° C)
Tank length:	24 in (61 cm)
Location in tank:	Middle
Foods:	Flake and small live foods.
Sexual dimorphism:	Male is slimmer, more colorful.
Breeding:	Yes
Comments:	A quiet, peaceful species that does best in schools. Should be kept with other small community fish.

Common name:	**Harlequin Rasbora**
Scientific name:	*Rasbora heteromorpha*
Family:	Cyprinidae
Origin:	Southeast Asia
Length of fish:	1.75 in (4 cm)
Temperature:	72–78° F (22°–25° C)
Tank length:	24 in (61 cm)
Location in tank:	Middle
Foods:	Flake and small live foods.
Sexual dimorphism:	Front edge of markings rounded at bottom in male.
Breeding:	Yes
Comments:	Should be kept in large groups of eight or more with other active but peaceful species.

Common name:	**Red-line Rasbora**
Scientific name:	*Rasbora pauciperforata*
Family:	Cyprinidae
Origin:	Southeast Asia
Length of fish:	3 in (7 cm)
Temperature:	72°–78° F (22°–25° C)
Tank length:	30 in (76 cm)
Location in tank:	Middle
Foods:	Flake and live foods; vegetable material.
Sexual dimorphism:	Male is larger.
Breeding:	Yes
Comments:	A lively fish that should be kept with other fast-swimming species. As with other barbs, maintain in small groups of at least three to five fish.

Common name:	**Scissor-tail Rasbora**
Scientific name:	*Rasbora trilineata*
Family:	Cyprinidae
Origin:	Southeast Asia
Length of fish:	6 in (15 cm)
Temperature:	72°–78° F (22°–25° C)
Tank length:	36 in (91 cm)
Location in tank:	Middle
Foods:	Flake and live foods.
Sexual dimorphism:	Male is smaller, slimmer.
Breeding:	Yes
Comments:	Active swimmer that should be kept in schools with fish of similar size and temperament.

Common name:	**White Cloud Mountain Minnow**
Scientific name:	*Tanichthys albonubes*
Family:	Cyprinidae

Origin:	China
Length of fish:	1.5 in (4 cm)
Temperature:	64°–72° F (18°–22° C)
Tank length:	24 in (61 cm)
Location in tank:	All
Foods:	Flake and live foods.
Sexual dimorphism:	Male is slimmer, more colorful.
Breeding:	Yes
Comments:	A hardy, peaceful fish well suited to a community tank containing other species of quiet disposition.

Common name:	**Marbled Hatchetfish**
Scientific name:	*Carnegiella strigata*
Family:	Gasteropelecidae
Origin:	Peru
Length of fish:	1.5 in (4 cm)
Temperature:	74°–82° F (24°–28° C)
Tank length:	30 in (76 cm)
Location in tank:	Top
Foods:	Flake and live foods.
Sexual dimorphism:	Female is deeper-bodied.
Breeding:	Yes
Comments:	Can be kept in community tanks but should be in groups of six or more of its kind. Fast swimmers, but peaceful.

Common name:	**Silver Hatchetfish**
Scientific name:	*Gasteropelecus sternicla*
Family:	Gasteropelecidae
Origin:	South America
Length of fish:	3.5 in (9 cm)
Temperature:	74°–86° F (23°–30° C)
Tank length:	48 in (122 cm)
Location in tank:	Middle-Top
Foods:	Flake and live foods.
Sexual dimorphism:	Unknown
Breeding:	No
Comments:	This species requires a large amount of swimming space. Should be kept in schools in community tanks. Excellent jumper, so tank covers are essential.

Common name: **Celebes Halfbeak**
Scientific name: *Nomorhamphus liemi liemi*

Family:	Hemirhamphidae
Origin:	South Celebes
Length of fish:	3.5 in (9 cm)
Temperature:	74°–80° F (23°–26° C)
Tank length:	30 in (76 cm)
Location in tank:	Top
Foods:	Flake and small live foods.
Sexual dimorphism:	Male is smaller, with black fleshy lobe on lower beak.
Breeding:	Yes
Comments:	Should be kept in schools. Does well in community aquariums, but must have excellent filtration and sufficient room—at least 20 gallons (76 l).

Common name:	**Golden Pencilfish**
Scientific name:	*Nannostomus beckfordi*
Family:	Lebiasinidae
Origin:	Guyana
Length of fish:	2.5 in (6 cm)
Temperature:	74°–80° F (23°–26° C)
Tank length:	24 in (61 cm)
Location in tank:	Middle-Top
Foods:	Flake and small live foods.
Sexual dimorphism:	Male is slimmer, with white tips on fins.
Breeding:	Yes
Comments:	A quiet, peaceful species that is recommended for community tanks as long as other fish are of similar temperament.

Common name:	**Three-lined Pencilfish**
Scientific name:	*Nannostomus trifasciatus*
Family:	Lebiasinidae
Origin:	Brazil
Length of fish:	1.5 in (4 cm)
Temperature:	74°–80° F (23°–26° C)
Tank length:	24 in (61 cm)
Location in tank:	Middle-Top
Foods:	Flake and small live foods.
Sexual dimorphism:	Female has rounder body.
Breeding:	Yes
Comments:	Does well with other small, peaceful community fish. Setups for all pencilfish should have hiding places and a central swimming area.

Common name:	**Guppy**
Scientific name:	*Poecilia reticulata*
Family:	Poeciliidae
Origin:	Central America and Brazil
Length of fish:	2.5 in (6 cm)
Temperature:	64°–82° F (18°–28° C)
Tank length:	24 in (61 cm)
Location in tank:	Middle-Top
Foods:	Flake and small live foods.
Sexual dimorphism:	Male is smaller, more colorful; has gonopodium (modified anal fin).
Breeding:	Yes
Comments:	Very popular, hardy community fish. Selective breeding has resulted in a wide variety of colors, patterns, and finnage.

Common name:	**Black Molly**
Scientific name:	*Poecilia* sp.
Family:	Poeciliidae
Origin:	Mexico and Central America
Length of fish:	2.5 in (6 cm)
Temperature:	64°–82° F (18°–28° C)
Tank length:	24 in (61 cm)
Location in tank:	Middle-Top
Foods:	Vegetable material, algae, flake foods.
Sexual dimorphism:	Male has gonopodium (modified anal fin).
Breeding:	Yes
Comments:	Peaceful community fish. Easiest of the mollies to keep, but not long-lived (perhaps three years).

Common name:	**Swordtail**
Scientific name:	*Xiphophorus helleri*
Family:	Poeciliidae
Origin:	Central America
Length of fish:	4.5 in (12 cm)
Temperature:	64°–82° F (18°–28° C)
Tank length:	24 in (61 cm)
Location in tank:	Middle-Top
Foods:	Flake and live foods.
Sexual dimorphism:	Male has "sword" and gonopodium (modified anal fin).
Breeding:	Yes
Comments:	A peaceful community tank resident, but requires very good water quality. Excellent jumper, so tank must be covered, with no openings in hood. Selective breeding has resulted in numerous colors and patterns.

Common name:	**Platy**
Scientific name:	*Xiphophorus maculatus*
Family:	Poeciliidae
Origin:	Mexico and Central America
Length of fish:	2.5 in (6 cm)
Temperature:	64°–78° F (18°–25° C)
Tank length:	24 in (61 cm)
Location in tank:	Middle
Foods:	Flake and live foods.
Sexual dimorphism:	Male is smaller, more colorful; has gonopodium (modified anal fin).
Breeding:	Yes
Comments:	A very peaceful community tank fish. Bred for a wide range of colors, patterns, and finnage.

Common name: **Variegated Platy**
Scientific name: *Xiphophorus variatus*
Family: Poeciliidae
Origin: Mexico
Length of fish: 2.5 in (6 cm)
Temperature: 60°–78° F (15°–25° C)
Tank length: 24 in (61 cm)
Location in tank: Middle-Top
Foods: Vegetable flake foods, vegetable material, algae.
Sexual dimorphism: Male has gonopodium (modified anal fin).
Breeding: Yes
Comments: An excellent addition to any community tank containing other peaceful fish, particularly those preferring cooler water.

Common name: **Madagascar Rainbowfish**
Scientific name: *Bedotia geayi*
Family: Atherinidae
Origin: Madagascar
Length of fish: 6 in (15 cm)
Temperature: 68°–76° F (20°–24° C)
Tank length: 30 in (76 cm)
Location in tank: Middle-Top
Foods: Flake and live foods.
Sexual dimorphism: Male is more colorful; dorsal fin is pointed.
Breeding: Yes
Comments: A quiet, peaceful species that can be kept in a community tank containing fish of similar disposition. Should be kept in schools.

Common name:	**Dwarf Rainbowfish**
Scientific name:	*Melanotaenia maccullochi*
Family:	Melanotaeniidae
Origin:	Australia
Length of fish:	3 in (7 cm)
Temperature:	68°–78° F (20°–25° C)
Tank length:	30 in (76 cm)
Location in tank:	Middle-Top
Foods:	Flake and live foods.
Sexual dimorphism:	Male has brighter colors, longer tail fin.
Breeding:	Yes
Comments:	An active but peaceful schooling fish that can be kept in a community aquarium with other suitable species. Water quality must be excellent.

Common name:	**Butterflyfish**
Scientific name:	*Pantodon buchholzi*

Family:	Pantodontidae
Origin:	West Africa
Length of fish:	4 in (10 cm)
Temperature:	72°–86° F (22°–30° C)
Tank length:	30 in (76 cm)
Location in tank:	Top
Foods:	Flake and live foods.
Sexual dimorphism:	Back edge of anal fin in male is curved.
Breeding:	Yes
Comments:	Can be kept in community tank as long as there are no other surface-dwelling fish or very small fish in aquarium.

SUGGESTED READING

There are many aquarium books on the market, and they vary in the quality and accuracy of information, as well as in the quality of the pictures. The list below is short but contains some of the best works currently available. If you want to become more involved in the hobby, reading about it is an excellent way to learn more about aquariums and fishkeeping.

A Fishkeeper's Guide to Community Fishes by Dick Mills. Tetra Press, 1985.

A Fishkeeper's Guide to Maintaining a Healthy Aquarium by Neville Carrington. Tetra Press, 1985.

A Fishkeeper's Guide to the Tropical Aquarium by Dick Mills. Tetra Press, 1984.

Aquarium Atlas by Rudiger Riehl and Hans A. Baensch. Tetra Press, 1987.

The Aquarium Fish Survival Manual by Brian Ward. Barron's, 1985.

The New Aquarium Handbook by Ines Scheurmann. Barron's, 1986.

The Manual of Fish Health by Chris Andrews, Adrian Exell, and Neville Carrington. Tetra Press, 1989.

INDEX